The
FIVE PROMISES
of BAPTISM

The
FIVE PROMISES
of BAPTISM

How to Understand Them and Make Them Real

by Father David M. Knight

➕ **ABBEY PRESS** Publications
1 Hill Drive
St. Meinrad, IN 47577

TABLE OF CONTENTS

Introduction: *The Invitation*

This is a book about promises.

Promises made to you by God, and how you can enter into them. Promises made to God by you, and how you can fulfill them. The promises of Baptism.

All of the Good News is enfolded in the mystery of Baptism. If we understand Baptism we will understand what Jesus came to do—and what we are called on and empowered to do as "members of his body" and sharers in his divine life.

The goal of this book is to help you understand, appreciate, and live the five mysteries, the five promises inherent in your Baptism.

This book will show you a simple—but meaningful—way to make your religion your way of life. To do it by simply making it your conscious focus in life to live out your Baptism.

Baptism is something all "spiritualities" in the Church have in common. A "spirituality" is simply a particular insightful way to live the life of grace "to the full."

The foundation of every spirituality in the Church is Baptism. That is just another way of saying that the foundation and goal of them all is living the "life of grace." Baptism is the sacrament that gave us a share in the divine life of God: the mystery we call "grace."

Baptism immersed us in five mysteries inherent in the life of grace. And explicitly committed us to living them out for the rest of our lives. No spirituality can ignore any one of the five consecrations and commitments of Baptism and be authentic. Every spirituality in the Church, and every particular "way of life," necessarily includes them.

But sometimes they are not made the focus of explicit notice. And sometimes they are not sufficiently explained.

This book hopes to remedy that and so enrich the spiritual life and spirituality of every person in the Church. So let's ask the question that rules them all:

What were you promised at Baptism? Do you experience those promises as being fulfilled in your life? If not, how can you make that happen?

The First Promise of Baptism
A New Identity

"It is no longer I who live,
but it is Christ who lives in me."

The first thing God promised you at Baptism was a new identity. He promised you would be "transfigured"—made glorious, something like the way Jesus was transfigured on the mountaintop.

> Jesus took with him Peter and James and his brother John and led them up a high mountain by themselves. And he was transfigured before them, and his face shone like the sun, and his clothes became dazzling white. . . . Suddenly a bright cloud overshadowed them, and from the cloud a voice said, "This is my Son, the Beloved; with him I am well pleased" (*Matthew* 17:1-5).

When Jesus was transfigured on the mountain, he wasn't changed. He was already divine. His glory just became visible. And the Father identified him as his "Beloved Son."

When you were "transfigured" at Baptism, however, you were changed. You became divine. But the glory of this did not become visible. In appearance you were the same. But in fact you became the "beloved son," the "beloved daughter" of the Father.

You became Christ.[1]

Suppose at your Baptism that change had become visible. Suppose the glory of your divinity—of the divine life within you, given to you at Baptism—had shone out, just for a few seconds. Suppose all present had seen your face "shining like the sun" and heard the Father's voice speaking out of a bright cloud that overshadowed them: "This is my son, my daughter, the beloved, on whom my favor rests."

Would anyone ever have looked on you in the same way again?

---

[1] This is the teaching of St. Augustine, quoted by John Paul II in *The Splendor of Truth*, no. 21: Having become one with Christ, the Christian "becomes a member of his Body, which is the Church" (*1 Corinthians* 12:13, 27). By the work of the Spirit, Baptism radically configures the faithful to Christ in the Paschal Mystery of death and resurrection; it "clothes him" in Christ (*Galatians* 3:27): "Let us rejoice and give thanks," exclaims Saint Augustine speaking to the baptized, "for we have become not only Christians, but Christ. Marvel and rejoice: we have become Christ!"

Would your image of yourself be different? Would your Baptism be something you would celebrate as the turning point of your life, the most significant day in your existence?

The day you received a new identity. The day you became Christ.

On the day you received your new identity—the day you were incorporated into Christ as a member of his body and became, in him, a true son or daughter of the Father and a "temple of the Holy Spirit"—the first promise of your Baptism was fulfilled. But to enter fully into that promise, you have to understand what it includes. What does it mean to "become Christ"? What does it empower you to do? What experiences of "life to the full" does it open to you? How does it change what you are in the eyes of God? In your own eyes? To what does it entitle you? To what does it commit you? And what other promises accompany this new identity?

The phrase, "You became Christ" may have shocked you. If so, it just bears out the point that something may have been lacking in the way we were evangelized. Four of the last popes have expressed concern that the Christians of today may not have really heard the Good News. Four popes have called for a "New Evangelization."

To quote just one of them, John Paul II called us to set ourselves and the world on fire again:

> Over the years, I have often repeated the summons to the new evangelization. I do so again now. We need to rekindle in ourselves the driving force of the beginnings and allow ourselves to be filled with the ardor of the apostolic preaching which followed Pentecost.[2]

We have "become Christ."

The first promise of Baptism sounds like the first and most fundamental temptation of the human race: the promise Satan made to Adam and Eve in the garden: "You will be like God."

The temptation was so strong because, in fact, this is what human beings were created for. The mistake—and sin—of Adam and Eve was not in wanting to be like God, but in wanting to achieve this in their own way, by their own power.

To "be like God" is the fruit of "grace," a word that means simply "gift." The "grace of our Lord Jesus Christ" is the gift of sharing in

---

[2]John Paul II, *At the Beginning of the New Millenium*, January 6, 2001, par. 40.

God's divine life. It is the gift of "becoming God." This is the first promise of Baptism. This is what Baptism gives.

The basic mystery of Baptism is that through this immersion we "become Christ." These are not words we are used to. What do they mean?

St. Augustine says, speaking to the baptized, "Let us rejoice and give thanks, for we have become not only Christians, but Christ. Marvel and rejoice: we have become Christ!"[3]

Fr. Michael Casey, a Trappist monk of Tarrawarra in Australia, says it more strongly than that in his book, *Fully Human, Fully Divine*:

> According to the teaching of many Church Fathers, particularly those of the East, Christian life consists not so much in being good as in becoming God. We have been reborn [through Baptism] into a different sphere of existence. We are products of God's new act of creation. . . . [Christian life is] a journey to become fully human and fully divine.

St. Paul brings it down to daily living:

> It is no longer I who live, but it is Christ who lives in me.

> As you therefore have received Christ Jesus the Lord, continue to live your lives in him.

> For to me, living is Christ and dying is gain (*Galatians* 2:20).

The mystery of our Baptism is that through incorporation into the body that died on the cross, we died with Christ and in Christ. Then we rose with him and in him to live now, not as what we were, but as the living body of Christ himself.

To explain that is the task of this chapter.

BAPTISM IS DYING AND RISING

Catholics believe in Baptism by immersion, even though for purposes of practicality we often sacrifice this rich symbolism for the less expressive practice of pouring.

Because of this mitigated but customary gesture, we think of Baptism as "washing away sins." That is to understate Christianity from the outset.

---

[3]Quoted by John Paul II in *The Splendor of Truth*, no. 21.

You can't really "wash away" sins, even though this is a time-honored description of Baptism straight out of Scripture. Sins are not washable; they are a part of our history. We cannot "wash away" something that has become part of our being.

Besides that, Baptism is not primarily about sin, any more than Jesus is primarily about forgiveness. Jesus came that we might "have life, and have it to the full." Baptism is about new life. Baptism is the end of one life and the beginning of another.

We go down into the waters of Baptism to die. We express, and we accept, that by going down into the water of Baptism as into the grave, we are giving up the life we enjoy here and now in order to emerge from those waters reborn into a new life received under an entirely new set of terms.

> So if anyone is in Christ, there is a new creation: everything old has passed away; see, everything has become new!
>
> You were taught to put away your former way of life, your old self . . . and to be renewed in the spirit of your minds, and to clothe yourselves with the new self, created according to the likeness of God in true righteousness and holiness.
>
> You have stripped off the old self with its practices and have clothed yourselves with the new self, which is being renewed in knowledge according to the image of its creator. In that renewal. . . . Christ is all and in all!
>
> As many of you as were baptized into Christ have clothed yourselves with Christ. There is no longer Jew or Greek, there is no longer slave or free, there is no longer male and female; for all of you are one in Christ Jesus.[4]

We "die in Christ" in order to "rise with Christ." At Baptism we (with all of our sins, past and future) are incorporated into the body of Jesus hanging on the cross—hanging there in the present, in the eternal "now" of God's time, although in our time frame it happened two thousand years ago. We are immersed in Christ as we are immersed in the water. When Christ dies, we die in him. We are buried with him, and our sins are annihilated. When Jesus rises, we rise with him and in him to live now, no longer as the selves we were, but as the risen body of Christ. We are a "new creation."

---

[4] *2 Corinthians* 5:17; *Ephesians* 4:22-24; *Colossians* 3:10; *Galatians* 3:27-28.

Baptism "Takes Away" Sin

The mystery of our redemption is not that God simply "forgives" us. Forgiveness does not take away guilt. If forgiveness brings about any change, the change is in the one who forgives—who becomes more loving by that act. The one who is forgiven remains the same. Forgiveness does not take away guilt; it just chooses to overlook it. That is why people who have killed or done serious damage to others do not always find peace, even after receiving forgiveness in the sacrament of Reconciliation. They say, "I am still the one who did what I did. I am glad God forgives me, but I can't forgive myself." Their error lies in not understanding that Jesus does not just forgive. He is the "Lamb of God" who in his death "takes away" our sin. It ceases to be part of our history. We no longer have any sins in our past. The one who committed those sins died, and we are a "new creation." This is a mystery we need to understand and appreciate.

In Baptism our "old self was crucified with Christ so that the body of sin might be destroyed." When Christ died, we died in him. When Christ rose, we rose with him and in him. We rose out of the waters of Baptism with our sins not just forgiven, but "taken away." All our sins and guilt—any action of our lives that was incorporated into the body that "became sin" on the cross—is taken out of our history, out of our past, in the only way that any action of our past can be taken away: by the ending of our history in death. More precisely, by the obliteration of our sinful history in the death of the "Lamb of God."[5]

Do you not know that all of us who have been baptized into Christ Jesus were baptized into his death? Therefore we have been buried with him by Baptism into death, so that, just as Christ was raised from the dead by the glory of the Father, so we too might walk in newness of life. For if we have been united with him in a death like his, we will certainly be united with him in a resurrection like his. We know that our old self was crucified with him so that the body of sin might be destroyed, and we might no longer be enslaved to sin. For whoever has died is freed from sin.[6]

We are "saved" because at Baptism we gave our bodies to Jesus, with all of our sins. Our bodies became his; our sins became his.

---

[5]*John* 1:29; *2 Corinthians* 5:17-21.
[6]*Romans* 6:37.

When he died, we died in him. And so, when he sees us holding on to our guilt, he says to us, and he has the right to say,

> If you gave me your sins at Baptism, they are mine. Let go of them. I was "made sin" for you, and through my death and rising I was "made perfect" so that in me you might "be perfect . . . as your heavenly Father is perfect." As my own risen body on earth you have been made holy with the very "righteousness of God." If you keep clinging to your guilt you are robbing me of what I died to deliver you from.[7]

Through the mystery of our identification with Christ in his dying and rising, through incorporation into the death of him who "became sin" for us, we have "become Christ." We have become the very "righteousness of God."

> For our sake he made him to be sin who knew no sin, so that in him we might become the righteousness of God.[8]

If we gave our bodies, with all of our sins, to Christ to die in him, we also gave our bodies to rise with him. This means we gave ourselves in Baptism to be Christ's own living, risen body on earth. St. Paul wrote, speaking of Baptism:

> I appeal to you therefore, brothers and sisters, by the mercies of God, to present your bodies as a living sacrifice, holy and acceptable to God. . . . Do not be conformed to this world, but be transformed by the renewing of your minds, so that you may discern what is the will of God—what is good and acceptable and perfect.[9]

We "presented our bodies as a living sacrifice." This means that wherever our live bodies are, we are "sacrificed" to letting Jesus Christ live and act in us as he desires for the redemption of the world. Our bodies belong to him. They have become his body. In him we have become Christ. And in us he has become what we are: male or female, Jew or Greek, black or white, young or old, healthy or sick, genius or challenged, professional or laborer, even to the extent of making his own the physical and emotional woundedness that is in us because of our sin or the sins of others. Whatever we are, Jesus Christ says of us, "This is my body." And we answer, "Your flesh, given for the life of the world."

---

[7] *2 Corinthians* 5:21; *Hebrews* 5:9; *Matthew* 5:48; *2 Corinthians* 5:21.
[8] *2 Corinthians* 5:21.
[9] *Romans* 12:1-2.

The first promise of Baptism is that we will "be like God." By the act and fact of our dying and rising "in Christ" our sins are taken away, so that we, "being rescued from the hands of our enemies, might serve him without fear, in holiness and righteousness" as Christ's risen body on earth. We have a new identity. We have "become Christ."[10]

SUMMARY

The core mystery—and the first promise—of Baptism is that through Baptism we have a new identity; we have "become Christ."

In answer to the question, "What has Baptism done for you?" each one of us should feel comfortable saying, "Through Baptism I became Christ. This is my true identity, and the only full and complete expression of who I am."

The first practical response to this chapter is just to believe that I have truly "become Christ."

Because I am "in Christ," sharing his life:

- I have become like God. I have become divine.

- My body is Christ's own body on earth.

- I am a true son or daughter of the Father, because all who are "in Christ" are "sons and daughters in the Son."

- I have received the Holy Spirit, who is enlightening and empowering me from within.

- God himself "abides in me."

- I have "eternal life," "life to the full," because I share in and live by the divine life that is proper to God alone.

- I am an "heir of heaven," because God's home, the home of Jesus' Father and my Father, is my true home.

- All of my sins have been "taken away," and I have become the very "righteousness of God."

- Henceforth, wherever my live body is, I am "sacrificed" to letting Jesus Christ speak and act in me to give life to the world. "It is no longer I who live, but it is Christ who lives in me."[11]

---

[10]*Luke* 1:74-75.
[11]*Galatians* 2:20.

Do I believe this? Do I claim all of it confidently as my identity? Is this the way I experience my existence? Is it the way I consciously live my life? If not, then I am not aware of, or have not assimilated, the first promise of my Baptism.

That is worth looking into!

To Live Is Christ—Our Response

At Baptism God did not just make promises to us; we also made promises to God.

These should not be confused with the general rejection of sin, Satan, and "all his works and empty promises" that the whole congregation makes during the Liturgy of Baptism at the Easter Sunday Vigil Mass. This is sometimes called a "renewal of baptismal promises," but it does not make explicit what those promises are.

This book will do that.

The first promise that we make at Baptism is, like the first promise God makes to us, the core and condensation of them all. We promise to accept our new identity. This is a commitment to live as the Christ we have become.

St. Paul puts it clearly:

So if you have been raised with Christ, seek the things that are above, where Christ is, seated at the right hand of God. Set your minds on things that are above, not on things that are on earth, for you have died, and your life is hidden with Christ in God.

When Christ who is your life is revealed, then you also will be revealed with him in glory.[12]

This is simply to accept our new identity. To be authentically Christian we have to "die" to living life in this world according to ordinary human standards. In Baptism we gave up everything this world holds out to us, just as if we were dead. Then we came back to life again to live in this world under an entirely different set of terms. We came back to life to live as the risen body of Jesus.

---

[12]*Colossians* 3:1-4.

Henceforth we live only for what he lived for and wants to live for now in us. We live to continue his presence and his mission in the world. That is all we live for. Everything else that is presented to us as a possible object of choice—every job, every enjoyment, every relationship, every invitation to do anything—we evaluate in terms of how it will help us carry out the mission of Jesus on earth. There is nothing else to live for. We have died, and our old life was buried with Christ. We have been raised up with Christ to be his risen body on earth. Our minds therefore are set on whatever is important to him. That is what we live for. That and nothing else.

This is good news. It gives us new meaning and purpose in life: a meaning and purpose that are divine. It also commits us to living on the level of God. "If you have been raised with Christ, seek the things that are above, where Christ is."

Is this possible?

At first glance this strikes us as impossible. That is a normal reaction. It was the response that Jesus' first disciples made to several things he said. And the answer Jesus gave each time was essentially the same: "For mortals it is impossible, but for God all things are possible."[13]

That is fine in theory. But how do we deal with it in practice? To live with—and live up to—this first and fundamental commitment of our Baptism, we need to do two things:

1) Accept Jesus as divine.

2) Deal with him as human.

And we need to accept the fact that we cannot always deal with Jesus as divine and human at the same time!

Some explanation is needed here.

LIVING IS BEING CHRIST

To live as Christ we have to make Christianity—make our religion—our way of life. We have to be able to say with St. Paul, "To me, living is Christ" (*Philippians* 1:21). Our whole life must consist in living and acting as Christ. If we have "become Christ," it stands to reason

---

[13]*Matthew* 10:16-31.

we have to be Christ and act like Christ in everything we do. So there is no longer any distinction between our "religion" and anything else we engage in. Everything we do, we do as Christ. And because we do everything as Christ, everything we do is different. Everything we do has religious significance and value for us. In fact, that is the only significance and value anything has for us.

If something means nothing in the context of my life as Christ, then it means nothing, period. Each of us says, "To me, living is Christ. . . . It is no longer I who live, but it is Christ who lives in me!"[14]

ACCEPTING JESUS AS GOD

The problem is, if we accept the ideal just described, and accept Jesus as God, we are not going to want him around all the time! If we are conscious of being Christ, and of Christ's presence in us, we are liable to find that inhibiting—something like taking one's mother along on a date!

If I treat Jesus as God, I can never say "No" to him—about anything. But all of us know we are not ready to do that. All of us say "No" sometimes to things we know God wants us to do. Or we say "Yes" to things we know God wants us not to do. We aren't perfect.

The key is to want to be perfect. To accept Jesus as divine, and to accept God as God, we have to truly embrace the First Commandment from the heart: "You shall love the LORD your God with all your heart, and with all your soul, and with all your might."

But wanting is not always willing. I may truly—sincerely—choose to love God as All, but in daily life choose over and over again to give something else a higher priority than what God desires. St. Paul himself experienced this:

> I do not understand my own actions. For I do not do what I want, but I do the very thing I hate. . . . I do not do the good I want, but the evil I do not want is what I do. . . .[15]

This is the same Paul who said, "To me, living is Christ. . . . It is no longer I who live, but it is Christ who lives in me"! How do we reconcile being Christ with acting frequently as if we aren't?

---

[14]*Philippians* 1:21; *Galatians* 2:20.
[15]*Romans* 7:15-24.

Paul himself gives the answer:

Those who live according to the flesh set their minds on the things of the flesh, but those who live according to the Spirit set their minds on the things of the Spirit. To set the mind on the flesh is death, but to set the mind on the Spirit is life and peace.[16]

It's a matter of mind-set.

We try to live out in action the ideals we have set our minds on. If we don't try, of course, we are insincere. But we are not insincere just because we try and fail, even frequently. The rate of failure is influenced by many things, some of them external to us. And Jesus does not look primarily to our successes and failures, even in responding to his own teachings. Jesus looks to the heart. He looks at what we have set our minds on, what we desire in our hearts.

Jesus chose Peter to be the "first" among his apostles, and the "rock" upon which he would build his Church. But in word and deed Peter has more recorded sins and errors than any of the disciples. Peter is presented as a weak man, and even at times as a coward. But he loved Jesus, and Jesus knew it. For Jesus this is what counted.

To treat God as God we have to make it the "mind set" of our lives to "love the LORD our God with all our heart, and with all our soul, and with all our might." This is to accept the goal Jesus laid down for us: "Be perfect, therefore, as your heavenly Father is perfect. . . . If you wish to be perfect . . . come, follow me."[17]

If we set our hearts on this, God will forgive every fall and failing along the way. This is the mystery of God's "steadfast love."

THE MYSTERY OF GOD

The most characteristic trait of God's infinite love—and love defines God's infinite Being—is that he never gives up on us. He is steadfast in his love for us even when we fail and vacillate. If we accept God as God, we have to accept that trustng in his love is something we owe him. We owe it to God to love him with "all our heart." We also owe it to God to trust that he will keep loving us with all his heart while we are trying and failing to do this.

---

[16]*Romans* 7:25 to 8:6.
[17]*Matthew* 5:48; 19:21.

God is God. He has told us:

> My thoughts are not your thoughts, nor are your ways my ways. . . . As high as the heavens are above the earth, so high are my ways above your ways and my thoughts above your thoughts.

The context in which he said this was: "Turn to the LORD for mercy; to our God who is generous in forgiving."[18]

To accept God as God is to accept his "steadfast love" as something infinitely beyond our power to ask or imagine.

DEALING WITH JESUS AS HUMAN

Cardinal John Henry Newman has said that we cannot deal with Jesus as divine and human at the same time. It is essential to keep this in mind if we want to have a truly human relationship with Jesus. This becomes clear when we start getting down to practice.

To consciously "be Christ" all day, every day, we need to keep ourselves aware that Jesus is always with us, always in us, always trying to act through us in everything we do. One of the easiest ways to do this is to form the habit of saying the "WIT prayer" all day long: before every work we engage in, before every action we perform: "Lord, do this with me, do this in me, do this through me."

This is a very easy thing to do. A little initial work may be required to form the habit. You may have to use some "gimmicks" to remind yourself to keep saying this prayer—for example, associating it with going through a door (at home you can put a handkerchief on the knob to remind yourself), turning on the ignition in your car, sitting down at your workbench or desk (make WIT your password or screensaver), or putting a cross or medal where you will see or feel it. The key is to raise your consciousness, keep yourself aware of asking Jesus to act with you, in you, and through you all day long. Once you form the habit—whether you use the WIT prayer or some other means—it costs nothing to keep doing it.

That is, it costs nothing unless you keep remembering that Jesus is God! Then you may feel inhibited all day; under pressure to act

---

[18]*Isaiah 55:7-9.*

just like Jesus in everything you do; subject to added guilt when you choose to do something not good, or not as good as God would like it to be.

No one can live with that.

Imagine a couple on their wedding day, each saying to the other, "Darling, I love you so much that I will never say 'No' to anything you ask of me. I will do absolutely everything you desire, all the time."

How long could either one survive that?

In all human relationships, one of the "givens" is that nobody is perfect. We may pledge—and pledge sincerely—undying, unrestricted love for another. But there will be moments when we are just not able (or, to be honest, not willing) to live up to what we pledged.

We haven't renounced the pledge. We still embrace it from the heart and are committed to it. We just are not able or willing at this particular moment, in these particular circumstances, to do what we promised to do. That is human nature. That is human life. That is a characteristic of every human relationship. Anyone who cannot accept this fact cannot enter into a human relationship with anyone on a level as deep and demanding as total love.

This is true of relationship with Jesus. If he required as a condition for "living as Christ," living as his body on earth, the guarantee that we would never fail him, he would not have any body on earth!

So all Jesus asks is the "mind set," the deep, sincere desire and determination to love him as God, "with all our heart, and with all our soul, and with all our might." And then he says, "As long as you do accept me as God, deal with me as you would with another human being. Just give me forward motion."

Treat Jesus as a Friend

We can't treat Jesus as God and human at the same time—at least, not all of the time. If we tried to treat him always as God, this would be so inhibiting that soon we would find ourselves "forgetting" to keep him with us. We would just forget to invite him to some of the places we are going, or to take part in some of the things we are going to do.

Jesus is the Savior. He deals with sin. He took us, with all of our sins, into his own body on the cross. He was "made sin" for us. The best thing we can do if we are going to sin is ask him to come with us. He may not be able to actively participate "in us and through us" in what we are going to do, but he can keep what we do from being as bad as it might be. And he can heal and repair us when it is over.

SOMETHING TO PONDER

To ask Jesus to leave when we are sinning is like asking a doctor or nurse to leave the room when we are gushing blood or our bowels are erupting. The messier things are with us, the more we need the person whose skill is precisely in dealing with that; whose call is to deal with it; the one who knows how to clean up and cure the mess we are in. And wants to.

That is what Jesus does as Savior. When sin is going on, he wants to be in the middle of it, doing what he can to stop it or keep it from getting worse. He said, "Those who are well have no need of a physician, but those who are sick; I have come to call not the righteous but sinners."[19]

Why don't we take him at his word?

What is written above is the "worst case scenario." We needed to consider it because this is the problem people immediately jump to when they are told they have "become Christ," or that they should try to stay conscious of Christ's presence within them all day long. But the truth is, most of the time we are not determined to sin! Most of the time, if we remember to ask Jesus to "do this with me, do this in me, do this through me," we will try to do what he wants us to do. If what we were intending to do seems incongruous with asking Jesus to do it with us, we will quite often decide not to do it. And if we were intending to do something good, it is very likely we will get some insight and do it even better.

A SIMPLE SUGGESTION: THE *WIT* PRAYER

The simplest, easiest way to "be Christ" in everything you do— simple but not simplistic—is just to form the habit of saying the

---

[19]*Mark 2:14-17.*

WIT prayer. Every morning, as soon as you awake, offer your body to Christ as you did on the day of your Baptism, to be his body.[20]

If you are young and agile (and alone), do it passionately: kneel and extend your arms in the form of a cross. Otherwise, say before you get out of bed, before you even open your eyes, "Lord, I give you my body. Live this day with me, live this day in me, live this day through me. Let me think with your thoughts and speak with your words and act as your body on earth."

Continue throughout the day to pray before everything you do, all day long: "Lord, do this With me, do this In me, do this Through me." That is the WIT prayer. It is the easiest, simplest way to grow into "being Christ."

TO BE CHRIST IS TO BE THE MESSIAH

What is the goal of all this? Essentially, it is just to realize, to take seriously and try to live up to the mystery of our Baptism. To the mystery of our new identity, our true identity, as having "become Christ."

What does "Christ" mean? It is the Greek word for "Anointed," which in Hebrew is "Messiah." By Baptism we have "become the Messiah."[21]

Christ has no lips to speak with now but ours, no hands to comfort with but ours, no feet to travel with but ours. Where we go, he goes. Where we, the members of his body, do not go he cannot be humanly present. Jesus continues to be Messiah in us; and "in him" we are, and are called to act as, the Messiah in our time and place.

What does this mean in practice? In practice it means that we allow, and consciously try to allow, Jesus in us to "save" everything we are involved in. By acting with us, in us, and through us in everything we do.

---

[20]*Romans* 12:1-2.

[21]The anointing with chrism in the rite of Baptism for infants is called the "messianic anointing." It commits, consecrates, and empowers the baptized to continue the mission of Jesus the Messiah, the "Anointed One." The words of anointing are, "As Christ was anointed Priest, Prophet, and King, so live always as a member of his body." This is the "job description" of a Christian. See the *Rite of Baptism for Children*, "Anointing with Chrism," no. 98, and the explanation of this in *The New Dictionary of Sacramental Worship*, ed. Peter Fink (Liturgical Press, 1990), page 275.

What Needs to Be "Saved"

Everything in human life tends to "veer off" to destructiveness and distortion. Or to mediocrity. Or to just plain meaninglessness. Why is this?

It is not because people are inherently "bad." It is because all human beings live in imperfect cultures. There is no human society that has not been infected by false attitudes, values, and priorities. No culture that does not implant in its members inclinations, fears, and inhibitions that have a negative influence on behavior.

Every human action puts something into the cultural environment that never goes away. Every expression of attitude influences in some way the attitudes of others. Every affirmation or denial of value lived out in action has an effect on the values of others. This is a fact of life, a fact of human nature. Humans are built to live in society, and in every society they affect and form one another. For better and for worse. This is "cultural conditioning." All human beings are "programmed" to a greater or lesser degree by the society they live in. We are all caught up to some extent in the currents of our culture. We are constantly being nudged off course by distortions of truth toward behavior that is destructive.

In its negative influence this programming is the result of "Original Sin." From the first sin ever committed in the human race, individuals have continued to think up and put into action new "original sins," new and original ways to mess up human life on earth (and some that are not so original).

When enough people imitate a given behavior, adopting for themselves the attitude or value it expresses, that way of thinking and acting becomes characteristic of the "culture." Then it begins to be absorbed by others unthinkingly. Once it is perceived as what "everybody" thinks or "everybody" does, it tends to be taken for granted. It is accepted uncritically as true, good, and desirable.

In part this is because, in spite of all protestations to the contrary, very few people have the confidence or the desire to be "different" from everybody else. We feel more secure following the crowd. We don't like to take the risk of making personal judgments. So we just "go along."

The whole country has been devastated and no one takes it to heart. . . . From one end of the country to the other, there is no peace for any living thing.[22]

When Christ's words fall on the "beaten path" of culture, they don't make any impression. They don't even penetrate:

"A sower went out to sow his seed; and as he sowed, some fell on the path and was trampled on, and the birds of the air ate it up. . . .[23]

Has infection by the culture affected your life or the lives of people you know? How many beautiful relationships of love have you seen turn destructive and end in hostility and alienation? How many people have begun careers with the highest ideals and ended up as disillusioned, burned-out time-servers? Or cold-hearted self-servers? How many distorted attitudes and values are diminishing family life, social life, church life, business, and political life?

How many people settle for mediocrity and mediocre joy in life because they have come to accept that this is "just the way it is" and realistically all it can be? How many have "come to terms" with life and decided to settle for less?

Where does Jesus fit into this picture? What kind of "Savior" is he? Does he just save us "out of" this world without being able to save us in it? Is he only able to "get us to heaven" at the end of our lives, but unable to save our lives on this earth from veering off to destructiveness and distortion, mediocrity and meaninglessness?

Did he come to save us or just to salvage us?

When Jesus said, "I came that they might have life and have it to the full!" did he mean here? Or only hereafter?[24]

A MOMENT OF TRUTH

At this point we are invited to a crucial act of faith. One not to be taken for granted. Do you believe that Jesus Christ can save your life on this earth from everything in it that is destructive or distorted? Or just mediocre?

---

[22]*Jeremiah* 12:11-12, New Jerusalem Bible.
[23]*Luke* 8:5.
[24]*John* 10:10.

19

Your own life. Your real life. Your home life, school and social life. What you do and experience on the job. Or in church.

Do you believe, really believe, that by giving Jesus an active part in your life, by making him a part of everything you do, involving him in it, interacting with him all day long, you can "save" every area and activity of your life from veering off toward destructiveness and distortion, mediocrity and meaninglessness? That you can make it beautiful, joyful, and fulfilling?

Do you believe Jesus can actually "save" your real life? And save it here as well as hereafter?

Be real. Do you believe this? Think about what your family life really is; your social life, business life, religious life, civic life. Do you really believe Jesus can make these everything you want them to be? Or close to it? If you do believe he can, what are you doing that shows you believe it?

You might say, "I pray." And that is a good answer, a necessary answer. But it is not a sufficient answer.

PRAYER IS NOT ENOUGH

In dealing with Jesus as Savior, we make two mistakes.

The first is that we just won't believe he can save our lives on this earth from continuing to be what they have become, or from becoming what we don't want them to be. Typically, we count only on ourselves for this. Quite commonly this leads us to resign ourselves to just making the best of things the way they are, because we can't do anything about it.

Our second mistake is to think God will save the situation if we pray.

To say this is a mistake is not to downplay prayer. Of course we should pray. We need to ask God to help us. Jesus repeatedly told us to do this. We are crazy if we don't ask God to help us. We can even ask for miracles, knowing they sometimes happen. But praying isn't enough.

God doesn't save the world by just beaming down graces from on high. When he decided to save the situation on earth, he came down here himself. God took flesh as a human being in Jesus and dealt with people face-to-face, on ground level.

God then interacted with people physically, in and through his physical body. He spoke words, he touched, he smiled, he preached and taught, he argued, he showed the way by example.

During his life on earth Jesus healed only those who got close enough to see him, or approached to touching distance—unless he was asked to help by someone who did get within hailing range, like the centurion who asked him to cure his servant long-distance.[25]

Jesus was a contact Savior, a hands-on healer. He wrote no books and gave no television talks. When people wanted to know where to find him he said, "Come and see." When they wanted to learn how to live, he said, "Follow me." To the world-weary and those beaten down by life he said, "Come to me." Jesus came to change life on this earth through human interaction with people.[26]

If we don't interact with him humanly, there is very little he can do for us.

Jesus Saves By Interaction

It is through our interaction with other people that we get messed up—infected with distorted attitudes and values. So God chose to save us in the same way we got messed up. In Jesus, God came as a human being, in the flesh, to save us through physical, human words and actions that heal. He came to save us from the human words and actions that wounded us, from the effects of our human interaction with other people in society. From the distorted attitudes and values we picked up through our interaction with other people. From our "cultural conditioning." He came to do it by showing us an alternate way. By living out before our eyes another set of attitudes and values.

This means that if we want Jesus to save us we have to interact with him. If we want him to save any particular thing we are doing from veering off to destructiveness, we have to interact with Jesus while we are doing that particular thing.

Because we have "become Christ," we are charged to be the Messiah—to let the Messiah live and act in us. Whatever we want Jesus

[25]*Mark* 8:5-13.
[26]*John* 1:39; *Matthew* 19:21; 11:28.

to "save" in our lives or the lives of others, we have to let him do it by acting with us, in us, and through us when we ourselves are involved in the action or situation that needs to be saved.

This means we have to interact with him in our hearts in a way that lets him interact with others through our actions. As "Christ-bearers" we need to bear him into the marketplace, into our homes and family life, into our participation at church, into business and politics—into every activity and situation on this earth that needs to be "saved" from destructiveness and distortion, mediocrity and meaninglessness.

The choice to interact with Christ in a way that lets him interact with others through us is the choice to live up to our baptismal anointing as Messiah.

Three practical ways to do this are:

- Say the WIT prayer all day long. This keeps you conscious.
- Ask yourself in every situation, "How would Jesus respond to this?"
- Act. Have the courage to do what you think Jesus might be wanting to do in and through you, even when you are not certain. You will learn by trial and error.

WE ARE THE GOOD NEWS

If we have "become Christ," and if we are charged and empowered to continue the mission of the Messiah on earth, then we are Good News for the world.

Jesus came proclaiming the "good news of the Kingdom." Jesus preached that the Kingdom was "at hand" or had "drawn near," not just because a certain time frame was coming to its end, but because an event had taken place. An event which fired the starting gun on "the time of fulfillment." The Word was made flesh and was dwelling among us. Jesus "the Christ," the Anointed One, was born and his mission had begun.

The "Good News" of the Kingdom was Jesus himself. With the arrival of Jesus the Kingdom was already present, although still to be realized in its fullness.[27]

---

[27]See *Matthew* 12:28; *Luke* 11:20; 17:2.

And we are that Good News today. Not us, but Jesus in us. Jesus whose body we are. Jesus whose life is within us.

If any one of us finds it difficult to say, "I have become Christ," or "I am the Messiah," it might be easier to say (although it means the same thing), "I am the Good News."

We are sent to be the Good News. Wherever we are, and whatever we are doing, we should be good news: the Good News.

When we enter a room, light should shine. Where we work, joy should be in the air. Where hostility or indifference to others is present, we should inject love. Where there is confusion and anxiety, we should be a visible oasis of peace. Why? Because this is what Jesus did. To do this is to "evangelize" in both senses of the word: to announce the Good News and to make it real.

Evangelization is the commitment that follows from the first mystery of Baptism. This follows from our new identity as the continuing presence of Jesus in the world. Because Jesus is the Good News, and because we have "become Christ," the Church as a whole and every member of the Church exists to evangelize.[28]

We are sent to be the Good News in the world. Evangelization should be a way of life for us.

"LORD, WHAT SHALL WE DO?"

And how do we evangelize? How do we show we really believe Jesus can save our lives and the lives of others from anything that diminishes them? How do we make the Good News happen?

The best way to show you believe in the Good News of Jesus is to let him act as Savior—as Messiah—in you. Keep inviting him to act with you, in you, and through you in everything you do. Try, as his living body, to "save" every environment, every situation you find yourself in. All day, every day. Try to enhance the life of every person you deal with. Not you alone, not as if you could do it by yourself; but, by offering your body as a "living sacrifice" to God every day, all day, as you did on the day of your Baptism.[29]

---

[28]Pope Paul VI wrote in *Evangelization in the Modern World*, no. 14, "The Church exists in order to evangelize."
[29]Romans 12:1-2.

BE THE MESSIAH! BE THE GOOD NEWS

The minute you wake up, say, "Lord, I offer you my body. Live this day with me, live this day in me, live this day through me. Let me think with your thoughts and speak with your words and act as your body on earth." Say it all day long. All day, every day.

Jesus is the vine; you are a branch. Let his life bear fruit through you. Let your presence on earth extend his saving presence to every place you go, to every person you deal with, to every activity you are involved in. Be a "Christ-bearer" by "being Christ."

If you do this, you will enter into the first promise of your Baptism. You will accept—and experience—that you have received a new identity. You have "become Christ."

KEY POINTS:

- The first effect of Baptism, which is the foundation of all others, is to give us a new identity. By Baptism we become Christ.

- The mystery of Baptism is that it incorporates us, with all of our sins, past, present, and future, into the body of Christ on the cross. We die in him and rise in him as a "new creation."

- By Baptism we die to life in this world as we received it at birth, and we rise in Christ to live as his risen body in the world. We have no other goal or purpose on earth except to let Jesus continue his presence and mission in us and grow to "full stature" in us and in the rest of the human race.

- In Baptism we are anointed as Christ to share in his messianic mission as Prophet, Priest, and King.

- To accept our mission as Jesus-Messiah, our first commitment is to let Jesus as Messiah-Savior act with us, in us, and through us to "save" everything we are involved in from destructiveness, distortion, mediocrity, and meaninglessness.

QUESTIONS FOR REFLECTION AND DISCUSSION:

- Before reading this chapter, how would you spontaneously have answered if you asked yourself the question, "What am I?"

- How would you answer it now?

- What is the first promise of Baptism? What benefits are included in it?

- What reasons would persuade you the most to accept God's invitation to give up the life you received at birth and live instead the new life given in Baptism?

- Would you have any problem saying the WIT prayer all day long?

A SUGGESTED KEY DECISION:

Form the habit of reciting the WIT prayer on waking and before everything you do, all day, every day: Lord, do this with me, do this in me, do this through me.

The Second Promise of Baptism
Enlightenment

Are you experiencing "life to the full"? That is what Jesus came to give. And he gave you the beginning of it at Baptism.

Are you growing into that life in its fullness?

Jesus said to those who wanted "more" than just a mediocre experience of existence on earth, "Come, follow me!"

He invites us to be his disciples.

It would be a mistake, however, to think that following Jesus makes us disciples. A disciple is a learner, a student. To be disciples we have to be learning from Jesus. To be students we have to be studying.

If we are not learning from Jesus now, if we are not in some way still and significantly "studying" the mystery of his mind and will and heart through reading and reflection, through discussion with others and with Jesus himself in prayer, we are no longer his "students." We are no longer disciples.

The goal of this chapter is not to make you feel guilty! It is to help you believe in, experience, and acknowledge the mystical experience of enlightenment that was promised to you at Baptism.

Why sell our religion short? We are believers in him who said, "I came that they might have life, and have it to the full"! If we don't experience our religion as something exciting—as an experience of interacting in mind-blowing ways with him who said, "I am the Way, the Truth and the Life," then something is wrong.

Most likely, what is wrong is something very simple: we are not really disciples of Jesus Christ. You can't be a disciple, a student, of the Way, the Truth, and the Life without finding your life more exciting.

What was Paul's prayer for the Christians he converted?

I pray that, according to the riches of his glory, he may grant that you may be strengthened in your inner being with power through his Spirit, and that Christ may dwell in your hearts through faith, as you are being rooted and grounded in love.

I pray that you may have the power to comprehend, with all the saints, what is the breadth and length and height and depth, and to know the love of Christ that surpasses knowledge, so that you may be filled with all the fullness of God.[1]

This is the second promise of our Baptism. We accept it, and live up to our side of the covenant, when we dedicate ourselves to life-long study of the mind and heart of God as revealed in Jesus Christ. Jesus said:

"If you continue in my word, you are truly my disciples; and you will know the truth, and the truth will make you free."

Free to love. And to live for love. It's a consequence of being a disciple:

"By this everyone will know that you are my disciples, if you have love for one another."

This faith and love are the foundation of our hope:

"My Father is glorified by this, that you bear much fruit and become my disciples."[2]

Faith, hope, and love are our experience of the life of grace, "life to the full." This chapter will help you enter more deeply into all three.

At Baptism we ask for "faith." By "faith" we don't mean just a human choice to believe. For Christians, faith itself is a mystery. The "gift of faith" is the mystery of sharing in God's own act of knowing. It is (along with the gifts of hope and love) one element of sharing in the divine life of God, which is the definition of "grace."

That makes faith a mystical experience.

Faith is not just the adult human action of making up our minds to believe in Jesus and accepting him as our Savior in a personal act of choice. We have to perform this personal act, of course (if we are adult and rational enough to be able to exercise free choice), but that is not what "saves" us. We are saved by "grace," and grace is an act, a gift, of God. Grace is the "favor" of sharing in the divine life of God, which is a favor only God can give, and nothing we are able to do can bring it about. It is a free gift; something God gives us, something God alone can give us.

---

[1] *Ephesians* 3:16-19.
[2] *John* 8:31.

> For by grace you have been saved through faith, and this is not your own doing; it is the gift of God—not the result of works, so that no one may boast.[3]

The life of God is knowing, willing, and loving. By faith we share in his act of knowing. By hope we share by anticipation in his act of willing. By graced love we share in his act of loving. This is the mystery of divine life in us, the mystery of grace.

THE PROMISE OF FAITH

The gift of faith is an experience of divine enlightenment.

"What do you ask of God's Church?"

"Faith."

The candidate for Baptism could just as well answer. "Enlightenment." In fact, in the Greek Church, Baptism is sometimes simply called "enlightenment," because those who receive the gift of faith through it are enlightened in their understanding. This puts the focus on Baptism as the "sacrament of faith," the sacrament which gives us a share in the divine knowing of God.[4]

We share in God's own act of knowing by sharing in God's own life. And we share in God's life by "becoming Christ" through incorporation into his body at Baptism. In other words, faith is an experience of identification with Christ. Because we are "in Christ," we "have the mind of Christ."[5]

This is an experience of the Holy Spirit.

> By this we know that we abide in him and he in us, because he has given us of his Spirit.[6]

> When we cry, "Abba! Father!" it is that very Spirit bearing witness with our spirit that we are children of God. . . . And because you are children, God has sent the Spirit of his Son into our hearts, crying, "Abba! Father!"[7]

No one can rightly call God "Father" except God the Son. When Jesus said, "No one knows the Son except the Father, and no one knows the Father except the Son," he was enunciating a principle of metaphysics! To know God as God you have to be God. To know the

---

[3]*Ephesians* 2:8-9.
[4]For references see the *Catechism of the Catholic Church*, no. 1216.
[5]*1 Corinthians* 2:16.
[6]*1 John* 2:24, 4:13.
[7]*Romans* 8:15-16; *Galatians* 4:6.

Father as Father you have to be God the Son. God himself could not empower any creature to do this. To know God as he is in himself is what it means to be God! To enable any human to do this, God would have to make that creature God.[8]

And that is exactly what God does in giving us "grace." Grace is the favor of sharing in the divine life of God. Jesus seemed to contradict himself when after saying "no one knows the Father except the Son," he added, ". . . and anyone to whom the Son chooses to reveal him." The fact is, Jesus does enable us to know the Father; and he does it in the only way it can be done: by letting us share in his own act of knowing the Father. He does this by incorporating us into his body and sharing with us his life as God the Son made flesh. "In Christ" we know the Father as "sons and daughters in the Son."[9]

It may have shocked us when (in the treatment of the first promise of Baptism) Fr. Michael Casey cited, "the teaching of many Church Fathers, particularly those of the East," to say that "Christian life consists not so much in being good as in becoming God."

It may shock us more to read in the Liturgy of the Hours, "Those who by faith are spiritual members of Christ can truly say that they are what he is: the Son of God and God himself!"[10]

---

[8]*Matthew* 11:27.

[9]This mystery of incorporation into Christ is a basic theme of St. Paul's letters. He uses the expression "in Christ" or its equivalent 164 times. And 29 times he uses the prefix syn- in Greek ("co-" in English) to express our union with Christ, as members of his body, in what he did and we do. Fernand Prat, S.J., gives the list in his *The Theology of St. Paul*, tr. John Stoddard (Burns Oates & Washbourne, 1934), Vol. II, pages 18-20 and 391-395: "In Christ" we **co-suffer**: *Romans* 8:17; *1 Corinthians* 12:26; are **co-crucified**: *Romans* 6:6; *Galatians* 2:20; we **co-die**: *2 Timothy* 2:11; cf. *2 Corinthians* 7:3; are **co-buried**: *Romans* 6:4; *Colossians* 2:12; **co-resurrected**: *Ephesians* 2:6; *Colossians* 2:12; 3:1; we **co-live**: *Romans* 6:8; are **co-vivified** (returned to life): *Ephesians* 2:5; *Colossians* 2:13; **co-formed** (configured): *Philippians* 3:10; *Romans* 8:21; **co-glorified**: *Romans* 8:17; **co-seated**: *Ephesians* 2:6; we **co-reign**: *2 Timothy* 2:12; cf. *1 Corinthians* 4:8; are **co-planted**: *Romans* 6:5; **co-heirs**: *Romans* 8:17; *Ephesians* 3:6; **co-sharers**: *Ephesians* 3:6; 5:7; **co-incarnated** (embodied): *Ephesians* 3:6; **co-built**: *Ephesians* 2:22; **co-structured** (and connected): *Ephesians* 2:21; *Ephesians* 4:16; *Colossians* 2:19. And add *1 Corinthians* 3:9: we are **co-workers** with God (synergoi), quoted in Vatican II on "Missionary Activity," no. 15, and *2 Corinthians* 6:1: **co-working** (synergountes). See also Joseph Fitzmyer, S.J., *Pauline Theology*, Prentice-Hall, 1967, pages 67-70.

[10]Blessed Isaac of Stella in the *Liturgy of the Hours*, second reading, Friday, fifth week of Easter. Blessed Isaac adds some theological precisions: "What Christ is by nature we are as his partners; what he is of himself in all fullness, we are as participants. Finally, what the Son of God is by generation, his members are by adoption." But the precisions are just qualifications of the basic fact: that by "the grace of our Lord Jesus Christ" we are identified with Jesus and we become divine.

But this is the only way we can receive the enlightenment of Baptism. We have to "become Christ," so that "in Christ" we can know the Father by sharing in the Son's own divine act of knowing God. That is the gift of faith. That is what we ask for at Baptism. That is what Baptism promises. That is what Baptism gives.

MAKING REAL OUR PROMISE

The price of enlightenment, however, is a commitment on our part to continue our journey into the light.

From the beginning, Baptism was linked with discipleship. When Jesus sent his apostles out to baptize, he said to them:

> Go . . . make disciples of all nations, baptizing them in the name of the Father and of the Son and of the Holy Spirit.[11]

In the preparation for Baptism, the commitment to discipleship is explicit. After the candidates declare they are asking God's Church for faith, the celebrant asks further: "What does faith give you?"

The candidates answer, "Eternal life." Immediately the celebrant presents them with a copy of the Gospel, quoting the words of Jesus, "This is eternal life, that they may know you, the only true God, and Jesus Christ whom you have sent." He continues:

> If, then, you wish to become his disciples and members of his Church, you must be guided to the fullness of the truth that he has revealed to us. You must learn to make the mind of Christ your own. You must strive to pattern your life on the teachings of the Gospel and so to love the Lord your God and your neighbor. For this was Christ's command and he was its perfect example.
>
> Is each of you ready to accept these teachings of the Gospel?[12]

When those being baptized answer, "Yes," to this question, they are committing themselves to discipleship—to a lifelong study of the mind and heart of Christ through reflection on the Gospel.

---

[11]*Matthew* 28:19. Michael G. Lawler writes in his article on "Marriage, Sacrament of" in *The New Dictionary of Sacramental Worship* (Liturgical Press, 1990), page 809: "One of the most central affirmations of Christian faith is the affirmation of discipleship. Disciple is an ever-present New Testament word, occurring some two hundred and fifty times throughout the Gospels and Acts, and always implying response to a call from the Lord. By definition disciples are learners, and the disciples of Christ are learners of mystery."

[12]*John* 17:3 and *Rite of Christian Initiation of Adults* (Study Edition), Liturgy Training Publications, 1988, #52-C, page 23.

This is to take seriously Christ's promise and invitation:

"I do not call you servants any longer, because the servant does not know what the master is doing; but I have called you friends, because I have made known to you everything that I have heard from my Father."[13]

In an alternate version of this ceremony, candidates are told that they are entering into a "way," a "path," a "journey." Baptism is a commitment to seek progressive enlightenment.

You have followed God's light and the way of the Gospel now lies open before you. Set your feet firmly on that path. . . . Walk in the light of Christ and learn. . . . This is the way of faith along which Christ will lead you in love toward eternal life. Are you prepared to begin this journey. . . ?[14]

Immediately after Baptism, the new Christians are given a candle that has been lit from the Easter candle, symbol of Christ, and exhorted: "You have been enlightened by Christ. Walk always as children of the light. . . ." Christ's light is "a lamp to our feet and a light to our path." Faith is a light to guide us, a light to move by, a light that gradually unfolds.[15]

The Christian life is an ongoing journey into the light. The journey continues until we are perfectly one with him who "dwells in unapproachable light, whom no one has ever seen or can see; to him be honor and eternal dominion. Amen!" But we will see him, because "we are God's children [and]. . . . when he is revealed, we will be like him, for we will see him as he is."[16]

Until then, however, "the path of the righteous is like the light of dawn, which shines brighter and brighter until full day."[17]

This is a gradual transformation. When we were invited at Baptism to "present our bodies as a living sacrifice, holy and acceptable to God. . ." Saint Paul exhorted us at the same time:

Do not be conformed to this world, but be transformed by the renewing of your minds, so that you may discern what is the will of God—what is good and acceptable and perfect (*Romans* 12:1-2).

---

[13]*John* 15:15.
[14]Ibid, #52-A, pages 22-23.
[15]Ibid, #230, page 144; *Psalm* 119:105.
[16]*Timothy* 6:16; *1 John* 3:2.
[17]*Proverbs* 4:18.

Discipleship is an ongoing endeavor, a continuing transformation. It is a life-long commitment to keep trying to grow into total union of mind and heart and will with God.[18]

A COMMITMENT TO READ THE BIBLE

We may not have realized it, and it may not have been specifically pointed out to us, but at Baptism we committed ourselves to read the Bible!

This was never made an explicit law in the Catholic Church. The reason is that the Church was in existence well over a thousand years before the printing press was invented. There were very few books available. Copies of the Bible were priceless. People did not learn to read. So the Church did not command what was, for the vast majority of Christians, simply impossible.

But now almost everyone can read. And everyone can afford a copy of the Bible. So why would anyone who was exhorted at Baptism to "be guided to the fullness of the truth," and to "learn to make the mind of Christ your own," and to "strive to pattern your life on the teachings of the Gospel," not take for granted that daily reading of the Bible is an indispensable staple of the Christian life?

Does the Church have to make a law for us to recognize the obvious?

Is it not evident—although many will find it upsetting—that there is just as much obligation for Christians to read the Bible as to go to church on Sunday? Do we need a law of the Church to tell us that we should read the words of God?

If, as Saint Paul wrote, "Whatever was written [in Scripture] was written for our instruction," and written by God himself as an "operator's manual" for the life of grace, do we have to be saints or geniuses to see that we ought to read it?[19]

The Acts of the Apostles say that the people of Beroea "were more receptive" to the preaching of Paul and Silas because, in response to

---

[18]Most people, when asked what a "disciple" is, will answer, "A follower of Jesus." But the truth is that the word "disciple" does not mean "follower." It means "student." We are only disciples of Jesus as long as we are students of his. If we stop trying to learn from him, we cease to be disciples. And since there is no "graduation" until we die, when we stop being students of his, we are "dropouts." That is a major problem in Christianity. The world is full of Christians who go to church but who, in terms of discipleship, have dropped out as students.
[19]*Romans* 15:4.

their words, they "examined the scriptures every day to see whether these things were so." Does this say something to us? Do we do the same in response to the homilies we hear at Mass?[20]

If we go to Jesus as disciples, to learn from him as Teacher, do we not believe he will do for us what he did for the two he met on the road to Emmaus, when he "opened their minds to understand the scriptures"? Do we not think our experience will be the same as theirs: "Were not our hearts burning within us while he was talking to us on the road, while he was opening the scriptures to us?"[21]

THE EXPERIENCE OF THE HOLY SPIRIT

Discipleship is a commitment to pursue deeper and deeper enlightenment through the gift of the Holy Spirit.

> No one comprehends what is truly God's except the Spirit of God. Now we have received not the spirit of the world, but the Spirit that is from God, so that we may understand the gifts bestowed on us by God. And we speak of these things in words not taught by human wisdom but taught by the Spirit, interpreting spiritual things to those who are spiritual. Those who are unspiritual do not receive the gifts of God's Spirit, for they are foolishness to them, and they are unable to understand them because they are spiritually discerned.[22]

Ultimately, all Christian discipleship is a mystical experience.

And we need to claim it as this.

Discipleship demands human efforts; but it is not just a human activity, and it is not just a human experience. It is an experience of seeking and finding enlightenment from God.

The future Pope Benedict XVI, told a world gathering of catechists and religion teachers in Rome, December 10, 2000, that the "Following of Christ" is not just "a question of morality, but a 'mysteric' theme—an ensemble of divine action and our response."

We often fail to notice this. St. Teresa of Avila complains about it: "We always hear about what a good thing prayer is. . . Yet only what we ourselves can do in prayer is explained to us; little is explained about what the Lord does in a soul."[23]

---

[20]*Acts* 17:11.
[21]*Luke* 24:13-35.
[22]*1 Corinthians* 2:10-14.
[23]*Interior Castle I*, ch. 2, no 7.

St. John's Gospel makes us conscious that we can walk by the "light of this world," which is "darkness," or we can walk by a light that is given by God—light which came into the world in its fullness only in Jesus Christ.

> The true light, which enlightens everyone, was coming into the world.
>
> He was in the world, and the world came into being through him; yet the world did not know him.
>
> He came to what was his own, and his own people did not accept him.
>
> But to all who received him, who believed in his name, he gave power to become children of God, who were born, not of blood or of the will of the flesh or of the will of man, but of God.
>
> And the Word became flesh and lived among us, and we have seen his glory, the glory as of a father's only son, full of grace and truth.[24]

CLAIMING THE EXPERIENCE OF ENLIGHTENMENT

The fruit of daily Scripture reading is that we arrive at a moment when we know the light we are experiencing is from God. It is not just the natural light of our intellects, and not just the learned light of culture or religion. It is the Light that is Life, because it comes from the Life within us and leads to Life in its fullness.

When we are meditating on the word of God, asking ourselves questions and trying to answer them, God is also at work. God is suggesting questions, God is proposing answers. We may not experience this at the time as anything but our own thought process; but at some point, when we look back on it we realize we were "thinking above our head," seeing more than we could reasonably have expected to see. This is the common experience of those for whom meditation is an abiding element of life.

We also notice over a period of time that our life has changed. Our behavior has altered. We are on a higher plane of understanding, insight, appreciation, and action. Something has changed us, helped us to grow. And we know it was not just our human efforts. This is an experience of enlightenment and empowerment by God. It is not the experience of illumination at a particular moment of time. We are not aware of any shafts of light piercing our soul, any blinding bursts of insight. It is rather the experience of a before and after, of a

---

[24]*John* 1:9-14.

passage from one point to another without our being able to identify all the particular steps along the way.

Like the light of dawn, which begins to creep almost unnoticed across the earth before the sun is actually visible in the sky, the truth begins to dawn in our hearts. We are groping in darkness, and then at some moment we realize that for quite a while now we have been in light. We are seeing what we did not see before. It is a gradual process: "The path of the righteous is like the light of dawn, which shines brighter and brighter until full day." This is the promised work of God: "By the tender mercy of our God, the dawn from on high will break upon us."[25]

When we give ourselves to meditation, we give ourselves to the experience of God. St. Paul made it clear that there is more to Christian enlightenment than just intellectual knowledge:

> When I came to you, brothers and sisters, I did not come proclaiming the mystery of God to you in lofty words or wisdom. My speech and my proclamation were not with plausible words of wisdom, but with a demonstration of the Spirit and of power, so that your faith might rest not on human wisdom but on the power of God.[26]

This is a mystical experience! The gift of faith is a gift of light. What we know by that gift we cannot know without it. To believe in Jesus Christ, and to pursue greater understanding of his teaching through study, discussion, and reflection, is to experience the mystery of increasing enlightenment from God. This is the fruit of discipleship.

EVERYDAY DISCIPLESHIP—EVERY DAY

The life of faith is a life of conscious interaction with God. It is an "ongoing conversation." A two-way channel of communication between ourselves and God. We don't simply "address prayers" to God. In discipleship, our prayers have a return address. We don't just "talk at" God. We talk and we listen. And we listen to learn. We converse with God, dialogue with God, argue with God.

It is important to argue with God. If we just say "Yes" without really challenging what God says, we will never understand how God thinks or why he asks what he does. If we disagree with God, we need to confront that. Work it out. We take for granted that he is right,

---

[25]*Proverbs* 4:18; *Luke* 1:78.
[26]*1 Corinthians* 2:1-5.

35

of course. We never forget that the one we are arguing with is God: infinite Truth, infinite Love. But we do justice to God only by trying to understand with our human minds; to comprehend, to see and agree personally with what God says. God wants friends and partners who feel they need hold nothing back.

In the prayer of discipleship, we ask questions to find answers. We find them by thinking about our own questions, trying to answer them ourselves, using what God says in Scripture or what we see Jesus doing in the Gospels. When we ask questions about what we read in Scripture, God inspires the answers we come up with. (He also inspires the questions!)

There is no guarantee that all our answers will be inspired and right, of course. Martin Luther himself, when he saw where "private interpretation" of the Bible was leading enthusiasts among his own followers, is said to have commented, "Some of these people speak as if they'd swallowed the Holy Spirit, feathers and all!" No one should presume personal infallibility.

For those who are afraid of being misled, there is a whole body of literature available that shares what the saints and spiritual masters have learned down the ages about "discernment of spirits." We have the advantage of being in a Church with two thousand years of experience dealing with trials and errors—and successes—in facing the challenge of the Gospel. No one has to "go it alone."

Most often, however—and we are talking about "everyday discipleship" on a daily basis—what we conclude from the Scriptures about the mind and heart of Christ will be so clear and obvious—once we have thought about it—that there is no danger of error. When we read the Bible for personal nourishment, it is rare that we confront something that is controversial. When we do, it usually stands out like a red flag. Then, if the question is worth bothering about, we can consult scholars and spiritual directors.

The point is, we should not be afraid to talk to Jesus. He is actually a pretty good teacher, and he promised that the Holy Spirit would help us understand what he teaches.

When the Spirit of truth comes, he will guide you into all the truth. . . . [he] will teach you everything, and remind you of all that I have said to you.[27]

This is a promise of ongoing enlightenment.

---

[27]*John* 16:13; 14:26.

No Longer Servants, But Friends

In discipleship we go beyond (but do not abandon) prayers of petition and intercession. Discipleship is about asking God for enlightenment, not just for favors, although it is always good and acceptable to ask God for help in our daily needs. Discipleship adds another dimension to our prayer: the dimension of exploration into God.

Nor is discipleship focused on asking God for practical advice about what to do about things in our life that bother us. This too is legitimate, but it is not enough. Our meditations on the Scripture should not turn into a series of problem-solving sessions. Above all, discipleship is an effort to understand God. It focuses on the mind and heart of God. Our desire is to confront and reflect on the words of Scripture in order to understand how God thinks, who God is, what he desires, why he does what he does, and why he wants us to do what he proposes to us.

The goal of discipleship is friendship with God—defined here as a comfortable intimacy with God, familiarity with his way of thinking, appreciation for his values, being in recognized agreement with his desires, experiencing co-commitment to his goals.

We recall again what Jesus said at the Last Supper:

> "I do not call you servants any longer, because the servant does not know what the master is doing; but I have called you friends, because I have made known to you everything that I have heard from my Father."[28]

When our greatest desire and most constant preoccupation is to know God as revealed incarnate in Jesus Christ, we will have become disciples.

And we will know that the promise of our Baptism is being fulfilled:

What do you ask of God's Church?

"Faith."

"What does faith offer you?"

"Eternal life."

---

[28]*John* 15:15.

Jesus said:

"This is eternal life, that they may know you, the only true God, and Jesus Christ whom you have sent."[29]

This is the promise of Baptism that is fulfilled in discipleship.

A SIMPLE SUGGESTION

If you want to be a disciple, a first concrete step—simple but not simplistic—is to start reading the Bible every day.

Many will find this too much to commit themselves to. But here is an "offer you cannot refuse." It is so simple, so easy, that you will not be able to think of any excuse not to do it!

1. Get a Bible. Get an inexpensive edition that you are not afraid to highlight, to underline, to scribble notes in.

2. Put it on your pillow. Do not put it on the table by your bed; you will end up forgetting it is there! Put the Bible on your pillow, on top of your bed. That way you can never go to sleep without picking it up. (It is impossible to go to sleep with a Bible under your ear!)

3. Promise God—what? To read a chapter a night? Be real. To read a paragraph or two? Even that you will find too much on some nights. Make a promise you can actually keep.

Promise God you will never go to sleep without reading one line.

DON'T DESPISE WHAT IS EASY

You may think it is hardly worthwhile to read one line of the Bible a night. After all, how much good can that do?

Remember the story of Naaman, the commander of King Aram's army. He was rich and important. And he contracted leprosy.

Naaman was not a Jew, but one of his slave girls, captured in a raid on Israel, suggested he go to Elisha the prophet to be cured.

He did, taking with him "ten talents of silver, six thousand shekels of gold, and ten sets of garments" as a gift. When he came to the

---

[29]*John* 17:3.

house of Elisha, however, the prophet would not accept his gifts or even come to the door to talk to him. He just sent word through his servant: "Go, wash in the Jordan seven times, and you will be healed."

Naaman was furious. He went away, saying:

"I thought that for me he would surely come out, and stand and call on the name of the LORD his God, and would wave his hand over the spot, and cure the leprosy! Are not . . . the rivers of Damascus better than all the waters of Israel? Could I not wash in them, and be clean?" He turned and went away in a rage.

But his servants said to him,

"Father, if the prophet had commanded you to do something difficult, would you not have done it? How much more, when all he said to you was, 'Wash, and be clean'?"

So Naaman went down and immersed himself seven times in the Jordan, and he was healed.[30]

Reading one line a night may not be "immersing" yourself in Scripture, but it is a start. Don't spurn the idea because it is so easy. Because it is so easy, you will never have an excuse not to do it. If you do read one line a night, you are keeping your promise to God, and that will encourage you. That will keep you going.

Most folks I casually check with, some time after making this suggestion, tell me they actually read three or four lines, just because it is hard to stop in the middle of a sentence.

Do that. And when you finish, do not put the Bible on your bed table. You will forget it is there. Put it on the floor, on top of your shoes. That way you will have to pick it up again when you get up.

Read one more line and put the Bible back on your pillow.

This might sound minimal, but it may be more than you are doing now. And it will let God say a couple of words to you every morning and every night.

Believe it or not, that will change your whole life!

Try it and see.

You will experience the fulfillment of the promise of enlightenment that was made to you at Baptism.

---

[30] *2 Kings* 5:1-14.

Key Points:

- Jesus came that we might "have life" and have it "to the full." But we have to grow into it. We grow through discipleship.

- The word "disciple" means "student." To be Christian disciples, we must be studying—still—the mind and will and heart of God as revealed in Jesus Christ, his life, and his words.

- Baptism promised us the gift of spiritual enlightenment. "Faith" is not just a human act but a divine gift and a mystical experience.

- We experience enlightenment, not usually in dramatic moments, but in a gradual realization that, through reading and reflecting on God's word, we have come to understand better and appreciate more what Christ teaches. And we know this is a gift.

- Discipleship is a life of conscious interaction with God. An "ongoing conversation" between ourselves and God. We talk and we listen. We listen to learn. This goes on all day.

- The goal of discipleship is friendship with God—a comfortable intimacy, familiarity with his way of thinking, appreciation for his values, being in recognized agreement with his desires, co-committed to his goals. Jesus offers it.

Questions For Reflection and Discussion:

- How have you experienced enlightenment from God?

- Do you experience friendship with Jesus Christ? Describe it.

- Are you afraid to read the Bible? Analyze this.

- Why do Catholics consider it an "obligation" to go to Mass on Sunday but not to read the Bible? What do you think of this?

A Suggested Key Decision:

1. Get a Bible.
2. Put it on your pillow.
3. Promise God you will never go to sleep without reading one line.

The Third Promise of Baptism
Power

*"You will receive power when the Holy Spirit
has come upon you;
and you will be my witnesses . . ."*[1]

*"As Christ was anointed . . . Prophet . . .
so may you live always as a member of his body."*[2]

WE ASKED IN THE TWO PREVIOUS CHAPTERS:

- What was promised to you at Baptism? And, are you experiencing "life to the full"?
- Do you experience God's baptismal promises to you as being overwhelmingly fulfilled in your life?
- Do you know that you have "become Christ"?
- Are you experiencing your faith as the gift of divine enlightenment?
- And are you "making real" the promises you made at Baptism? Are you fulfilling your side of the bargain?

In this chapter we are going to look at something that happened to you at Baptism—something you were consecrated, empowered, and committed to do—that you may hardly ever have thought about.

Do you think of yourself as a prophet?

God does. God even anointed you solemnly at Baptism to be one. The words of the anointing were, "As Christ was anointed Priest, Prophet, and King, so live always as a member of his body."

Let's start with Prophet. What does it mean to be one? What did God promise you at Baptism when you were made a prophet? What did you promise when, in accepting Baptism, you accepted your consecration as "prophet"?

That is what this chapter is all about. Enjoy it!

---

[1] *Acts* 1:8; and see 8:15, 19; 19:2; *Galatians* 3:2.
[2] *Rite of Baptism for Children*, no. 98.

The invitation to Baptism in the apostles' first preaching promised forgiveness and the gift of the Holy Spirit.

> Peter said to them, "Repent, and be baptized every one of you in the name of Jesus Christ so that your sins may be forgiven; and you will receive the gift of the Holy Spirit."[3]

We have already seen that in Baptism our sins are not just "forgiven" but taken away in the mystery of our dying in Christ as the "Lamb of God" and rising again in him as a "new creation." We receive the gift of a new identity. We "become Christ." We are "clothed with the new self, created according to the likeness of God in true righteousness and holiness."[4]

We have also seen that at Baptism we receive the gift of enlightenment: the Holy Spirit is given to us. "The Spirit of truth, whom the world cannot receive . . . abides with you, and he will be in you."[5]

> "For once you were darkness, but now in the Lord you are light. Live as children of light. . . ."[6]

But before he ascended into heaven, Jesus promised to give us the Spirit in a new way. This is the Spirit of power.

Power to break free of slavery to cultural conditioning. Power to smash the idols in one's own life and to challenge the idols of society. Power to stand against the tide, to swim against the current. The power to be free.

> "You will know the truth, and the truth will make you free."[7]

Specifically, this is the power to carry on the mission of Jesus through prophetic witness.

> "You are witnesses of these things. And see, I am sending upon you what my Father promised; so stay here in the city until you have been clothed with power from on high."[8]

> "You are a chosen race, a royal priesthood, a holy nation, God's own people, in order that you may proclaim the mighty acts of him who called you out of darkness into his marvelous light."[9]

---

[3] *Acts* 2:38.
[4] *Ephesians* 4:24.
[5] *John* 14:17.
[6] *Ephesians* 5:8.
[7] *John* 8:32.
[8] *Luke* 24:47-51.
[9] *1 Peter* 2:9.

We don't carry on this mission alone. We continue it with Jesus. We are co-missioned with him. St. Paul calls us "co-workers" with each other and with God. We are "co-working" with Christ, who promised to be "with us always, to the end of the age."[10]

EMPOWERMENT FOR MISSION

The bishop's exhortation, during the ritual of Confirmation that completes Baptism, emphasizes the orientation of this sacrament to mission:

> You have already been baptized into Christ and now you will receive the power of his Spirit. . . . You must be witnesses before all the world . . . our way of life should at all times reflect the goodness of Christ. Christ gives varied gifts to his Church, and the Spirit distributes them among the members of Christ's body to build up the holy people of God in unity and love.

> Be active members of the Church. . . . Under the guidance of the Holy Spirit give your lives completely in the service of all, as did Christ, who came not to be served but to serve.[11]

The anointing with chrism in the rite of Baptism for infants is called the "messianic anointing." It commits, consecrates, and empowers the baptized to continue the mission of Jesus the Messiah, the "Anointed One." The words of anointing are, "As Christ was anointed Priest, Prophet, and King, so live always as a member of his body." This is the "job description" of a Christian. From Baptism on, every Christian exists to evangelize.[12]

This means that Baptism gives a new meaning and purpose to our lives. We are no longer on earth just to "praise, reverence, and serve God" in an unspecified way. We live now precisely to carry on the mission of Jesus the Messiah. We are anointed and empowered to do this. We are consecrated and commissioned to carry on the mission of Jesus as his living body on earth.[13]

Does this restrict our lives—or enlarge them?

---

[10]See *1 Corinthians* 3:9; *2 Corinthians* 6:1; *Matthew* 28:20.

[11]See the *Rite of Confirmation Within the Mass*.

[12]See the *Rite of Baptism for Children*, "Anointing with Chrism," no. 98, and the explanation of this in *The New Dictionary of Sacramental Worship*, ed. Peter Fink (Liturgical Press, 1990), page 275. REF. Pope Paul VI wrote in *Evangelization in the Modern World*, no. 14, "The Church exists in order to evangelize." This, then, is what each member of the Church exists for while on earth.

[13]See the *Spiritual Exercises of St. Ignatius of Loyola*, "First Principle and Foundation."

Carrying out the mission of Jesus excludes nothing desirable in our lives. It is not a specific type of work that excludes other work. It includes everything we are rightly inclined or committed to do. Our mission pervades and "leavens" everything else. Family life. Social life. Civic life. Professional life. Being focused on the mission of Jesus does not make us less focused on anything else but brings everything we do into a sharper focus of clarity, purpose, and value. Our life at home is divine. Our intention at work is divine. The level and tone of our social life is divine. Everything we do is divine, because we have the divine life of God within us. When this becomes visible—physically evident in everything we say and do—we are bearing witness to Jesus Christ.

AUTHENTICITY DEPENDS ON AWARENESS

Christ's life in us becomes visible in our self-expression. But the self we express is the self we are conscious of—even if this is often an underlying "sub" consciousness. The body is the outward manifestation of the soul. We express and live out in action what our hearts embrace in desire. This is our real self, the self we deeply choose and know ourselves to be—at least when we are being authentic. To keep ourselves conscious of what we most deeply desire is, then, a first principle of authenticity. Saint Paul declares it:

> So if you have been raised with Christ, seek the things that are above, where Christ is, seated at the right hand of God. Set your minds on things that are above, not on things that are on earth, for you have died, and your life is hidden with Christ in God.
>
> When Christ who is your life is revealed, then you also will be revealed with him in glory.[14]

If we remain conscious that we have "become Christ" and live out of that consciousness, he will be revealed in us here and now. And our true self will be revealed—to ourselves and to others. Our actions will "give glory" to Christ because they will make it manifest that Jesus is indeed risen; that he is alive and active and living now in us who are his body on earth. This is Christian witness. It is also the revelation of the power of the Spirit in us.[15]

---

[14]*Colossians 3:1-4.*
[15]See *John 17:4-26; 2 Thessalonians 1:11-12.*

Being a "Prophet"—Empowerment to Witness

In explaining the messianic consecration to mission, we will look at prophet first, the call to bear witness and evangelize. This is above all the experience of faith.[16]

To be a "prophet" means to "profess" the faith in such a way that we share the Good News with others. But this profession, to be effective witness, must be above all a profession in action rather than in words. Then, and only then, is it "evangelization." Pope Paul VI put it this way:

> Above all the Gospel must be proclaimed by witness. . . . The first means of evangelization is the witness of an authentically Christian life. Modern people listen more willingly to witnesses than to teachers, and if they do listen to teachers, it is because they are witnesses. . . . It is therefore primarily by her conduct and by her life that the Church will evangelize the world. . . .[17]

Witness Is Lifestyle

Christian witness is not a matter of trying to impress anyone. Nor is it primarily preaching or teaching, although these belong to the prophetic role. Witness is simply lifestyle. It is living as the Christ we are, as his risen body on earth.

Authentic witnesses are those who, at home and at work, in pleasure and in pain, when things are going well for them and when things are going badly, "radiate faith in values that go beyond current values, and hope in something not seen, that one would not dare to imagine." Again, the words of Pope Paul VI:

> "Through this wordless witness they stir up irresistible questions in the hearts of those who see how they live: Why are they like this? Why do they live in this way? What or who is it that inspires them? Why are they in our midst? Such a witness is already a silent proclamation of the Good News. . . . Here we have an initial act of evangelization."[18]

---

[16]Being "priest in the Priest" (and "victim in the Victim," offering ourselves with Christ and in Christ for the life of the world) is above all the experience of love. To continue Christ's mission as King, or stewards of his kingship, we need above all hope to persevere in efforts to renew society and the world.

[17]See Pope Paul VI, *Evangelization in the Modern World*: nos. 14, 21, 41.

[18]Pope Paul VI, *Evangelization in the Modern World*: nos.14, 21, 26, 41.

LEAVEN IN THE DOUGH

This divine power is promised and given to all the baptized. It is not something restricted to the clergy or given only to the exceptionally holy. The power we receive is not the power to dramatically "cast out demons" and cure the sick. It is the less dramatic but even more enduring power to roll back the tide of evil in the world and help bring the whole human race into the "fullness of life" that Jesus promised and came to give.[19]

This work is in a special way the call and commitment of the laity. Unlike the clergy, the laity are everywhere. The Second Vatican Council (1962-1965) defines the laity as Christians who:

> seek the kingdom of God by engaging in temporal affairs and by ordering them according to the plan of God. They live in the world, that is, in each and in all of the secular professions and occupations. They live in the ordinary circumstances of family and social life, from which the very web of their existence is woven.

And everywhere they are, everything they do should express and reveal the faith-vision in their hearts. This is the specific vocation of those called to be the "leaven" in the mass of humanity.

> They are called there by God, so that . . . being led by the spirit of the Gospel they can work for the sanctification of the world from within, in the manner of leaven . . . by the testimony of a life resplendent in faith, hope, and love.[20]

The key word is "resplendent."

THE SPLENDOR OF THE SPIRIT

The Jesuit poet, Gerald Manley Hopkins, saw nature itself as resplendent with the glory of God:

> The world is charged with the grandeur of God.
> It will flame out, like shining from shook foil. . . .

Hopkins recognized the defacement of nature by human abuse; he acknowledged, "All is seared with trade: bleared, smeared with toil. . . ." But he insisted nevertheless:

---

[19]See *John* 10:10.
[20]Second Vatican Ecumenical Council, Dogmatic *Constitution on the Church Lumen Gentium*, no. 31. See also *Decree on the Apostolate of the Laity Apostolicam Actuositatem*, no. 2.

There lives the dearest freshness deep down things.
And though the last lights off the black West went
   Oh, morning, at the brown brink eastward springs—
Because the Holy Ghost over the bent
   World broods with warm breast and with ah! bright wings![21]

The Holy Spirit is the beautifying power of God in the universe. The Spirit beautifies above all by "making all things new" in the heart and soul of humans who live by the life of God.

> Life in humans is the glory of God; the life of humans is the vision of God. If the revelation of God through creation gives life to all who live upon the earth, much more does the manifestation of the Father through the Word give life to those who see God.[22]

The "testimony of a life resplendent in faith, hope, and love" is a testimony to the renewing, beautifying, all-enhancing work of the Spirit alive and active in those who believe in Jesus Christ, and are enfleshing him as his living body on earth. If their lives are "resplendent" by a lifestyle that makes visible the divine light of their faith, their lifestyle makes visible the presence and power of the risen Jesus and of his Spirit on earth.

That is why the Church prays, adapting the words of the psalmist with clear faith and enduring hope: "Send forth your Spirit, Lord, and our hearts will be regenerated."

"And you will renew the face of the earth"![23]

THE NEW EVANGELIZATION

God has promised the "power of his Spirit" to "renew the face of the earth." The key to this renewal is witness. And the key to witness is awareness made visible in expression.

Saint Paul calls us to awareness:

> Do you not know that your bodies are members of Christ? . . . That your body is a temple of the Holy Spirit within you, which you have from God, and that you are not your own?

---

[21]Gerard Manley Hopkins, S.J., "God's Grandeur," *Poems of Gerard Manley Hopkins*, ed. W. H. Gardner (New York: Oxford University Press, 1948), p. 70.
[22]St. Irenaeus, *Against Heresies*.
[23]See *Psalm* 104:30 and *Revelation* 21:5.

You were washed, you were sanctified, you were justified in the name of the Lord Jesus Christ and in the Spirit of our God. . . .

You were bought with a price; therefore glorify God in your body.[24]

We have to work on our mindset:

If with Christ you died to the elemental spirits of the universe, why do you live as if you still belonged to the world?

If you have been raised with Christ, seek the things that are above, where Christ is, seated at the right hand of God. Set your minds on things that are above, not on things that are on earth, for you have died, and your life is hidden with Christ in God. When Christ who is your life is revealed, then you also will be revealed with him in glory.[25]

NEED FOR EXPRESSION

The world cannot wait until Christ comes for his "glory to be revealed." It has to be revealed now, on our earth, in our time and space, through the "testimony of lives resplendent in faith, hope and love." This is the way, and the only way, the world will be evangelized. Through Christian self-expression.

Jesus promised that we would "glorify" him by the visible witness of our lives on earth: "My Father is glorified by this, that you bear much fruit and become my disciples."

Jesus . . . looked up to heaven and said, "Father, the hour has come; glorify your Son so that the Son may glorify you. . . .

"I have made your name known to those whom you gave me from the world. They were yours, and you gave them to me, and they have kept your word. . . . they have believed that you sent me."

". . . They are yours. All mine are yours, and yours are mine; and I have been glorified in them."[26]

When the invisible life of grace in us becomes visible by "taking flesh" in our physical words and actions, the risen Jesus is revealed as alive and active in his body on earth, the Church.

The activities of divine life in us are faith, hope, and love. But invisible, these are not witness. Our faith becomes witness when we give

---

[24]See *1 Corinthians* 6:15-20.
[25]*Colossians* 2:20; 3:1-4.
[26]*John* 15:8; 17:1-10.

48

visible expression in words and actions to the invisible truth in our minds. We reveal the divine love in our hearts when we give expression to that love in physical interaction with others.

This witness is the work of the Spirit. It is for others the revelation, and for ourselves the experience of the "gift of the Holy Spirit."

THE EXPERIENCE OF THE SPIRIT

There is no doubt that in the early Church the gift of the Holy Spirit was a matter of personal, even visible, experience. Peter promised it: "Be baptized every one of you in the name of Jesus Christ . . . and you will receive the gift of the Holy Spirit."

The promise was fulfilled in a visible way when the apostles "laid hands" on the baptized:

> Now when the apostles at Jerusalem heard that Samaria had accepted the word of God, they sent Peter and John to them. The two went down and prayed for them that they might receive the Holy Spirit (for as yet the Spirit had not come upon any of them; they had only been baptized in the name of the Lord Jesus).Then Peter and John laid their hands on them, and they received the Holy Spirit.

In the early days this experience seems to have been associated with such charismatic expressions as "speaking in tongues and extolling God" in ecstatic or enthusiastic ways. When Paul laid hands on the Ephesians, "the Holy Spirit came upon them, and they spoke in tongues and prophesied." But this is not what ordinarily occurs in our time.[27]

The gift of the Holy Spirit is given, however. That promise is always fulfilled. And we need to take for granted that the Spirit is given in a way that can be experienced if we accept and enter into our Baptism as we should. So the question is, how do we experience the gift of the Spirit when it is given to us at Baptism through our "messianic anointing" as prophets, priests, and stewards of Christ's kingship?[28]

---

[27]*Acts* 2:38; 8:14-17; 10:44-48; 19:1-6.

[28]The Spirit is given anew in the "pneumatic anointing" that is part of the Rite of Confirmation. See *The New Dictionary of Sacramental Worship*, ed. Peter Fink (Liturgical Press, 1990), pages 275 (messianic, Christological anointing on the top of the head at Baptism) and 276-277 (pneumatic anointing by the bishop on the forehead at Confirmation).

"Little Children, Keep Yourselves From Idols"

The first way to experience the gift of the Spirit is to make a conscious break with the idolatry of our culture.

> Do not be conformed to this world, but be transformed by the renewing of your minds. . . . You must no longer live as the Gentiles live, in the futility of their minds. . . .
>
> For once you were darkness, but now in the Lord you are light. Live as children of light. . . . Live, not as unwise people but as wise.
>
> Set your minds on things that are above, not on things that are on earth. . . . Put to death, therefore, whatever in you is earthly. . . (which is idolatry).[29]

All of this is a realization of the new identity we have through grace, by sharing in the divine life of God.

> What agreement has the temple of God with idols? For we are the temple of the living God; as God said, "I will live in them and walk among them, and I will be their God, and they shall be my people.

We experience our new identity through and in the experience of a new freedom, which is ours by the gift of the Spirit. When we realize that we have declared ourselves free of slavery to our peer group and to our culture, this is an experience of having been set free by Jesus Christ. When we become explicitly conscious that we are determined to let God and God alone—not the culture, or any goal or value in this world—give direction to our lives, determine our priorities and motivate our choices, then we realize that for us Jesus is indeed "Lord." St. Paul says that to know this is to experience the gift of the Holy Spirit:

> Now concerning spiritual gifts, brothers and sisters, I do not want you to be uninformed. You know that when you were pagans, you were enticed and led astray to idols that could not speak. Therefore I want you to understand that . . . no one can say "Jesus is Lord" except by the Holy Spirit.[30]

Unless a real surrender in faith to Jesus as Lord has set us free—by the power of his Spirit—from slavery to our society's values, our society's priorities, compulsions, and inhibitions, we are still under the domination of "idols." The influence of a peer group—friends

---

[29]*Romans* 12:2; *Philippians* 2:15; *Ephesians* 4:1-20; 5:3-15; *Colossians* 3:2-5.
[30]*1 Corinthians* 12:1-3.

and family, fellow students and co-workers—is often so powerful that it can be enslaving. Whatever values we passively accept, without consciously relating them to the teaching and service of Christ, become like "idols."

When we know we have broken free of that idolatry, we know that we have in fact accepted Jesus as Lord—by the gift of the Holy Spirit. In turning away from idols we know that we know Jesus Christ. This is an experience of the "gift of the Holy Spirit."

> We know that the Son of God has come and has given us understanding so that we may know him who is true; and we are in him who is true, in his Son Jesus Christ. He is the true God and eternal life.
>
> Little children, keep yourselves from idols.[31]

"THEY WILL SPEAK IN NEW TONGUES . . ."

Once we are able to break free from such idolatry, we realize we have become "different" from others in our outlook. Jesus promised that those who receive the gift of the Spirit would become so different in their way of perceiving life that non-believers would say of them, "We are not speaking the same language."

> "These signs will accompany those who believe: by using my name they will cast out demons; they will speak in new tongues. They will pick up snakes in their hands, and if they drink any deadly thing, it will not hurt them; they will lay their hands on the sick, and they will recover." . . .[32]

We do indeed begin to speak in a way that no longer echoes the dogmas of our culture, in a "tongue" that is different from that of our peer group. We no longer see the world or respond to it the way others do. Because of this we acquire a certain "immunity" to the influence of the culture.

In our own lives—and with a growing influence on others and on our environment—we can begin to "cast out the demons" of violence, divisiveness, social discrimination, sexual and economic exploitation, nationalistic arrogance, and selfishness. We find we are able to "handle" the morally and psychologically destructive elements in our profession and social circle. We can "drink in" daily whatever may come to us

---

[31] *1 John* 5:20.
[32] *Mark* 16:17-18.

through the media, the advertisements for affluence, or through casual conversation, without being harmed by it. We are even able to touch the minds and hearts of others with whom we come into contact and help them "recover" from wounds they have suffered in our infected society. This is an experience of the power of the Spirit within us, the result of being freed from slavery to "idols" through the recognition of Jesus as "Lord."[33]

As this surrender to the lordship of Jesus Christ spreads throughout the Church, we will experience a "new Pentecost." We become like those present at the first Pentecost, who were "filled with the Holy Spirit and began to speak in other languages as the Spirit gave them ability."[34]

IMPULSION TO UNITY

A third way to experience the gift of the Spirit is to get into contact with an inner drive impelling us to desire unity with all people: with those in our family, with friends and associates, within the Church, with those of other religions, races, and nations.

This is the deeper meaning of the "gift of tongues" that was experienced at Pentecost.

When we recognize that "Jesus is Lord" and that our true nationality, our true "citizenship," is "in heaven," we will speak other languages. Or better, we will all speak the common language of the Spirit that unites all peoples in the People of God. The "gift of tongues" at Pentecost was a sign that, through the outpouring of his Spirit, God was going to re-unite the human race divided since the Tower of Babel. There pride and selfishness ignited the violence that forced people to separate into isolated clans that eventually could not communicate with each other. Through the Holy Spirit, the divisiveness caused by sin is overcome, and the family of the human race will come together again to live in the "unity and peace" of Christ's kingdom.[35]

---

[33]This is not a specific criticism of American society. Every human society is formed by countless billions of free human actions, good and bad. These form and establish a social environment that influences—in helpful and in destructive ways—every person born into that culture. This is the fruit of "original sin."

[34]*Acts* 2:4.

[35]See *Philippians* 3:20 and the *Communion Rite of the Mass*, prayer before the Sign of Peace.

Pentecost was the sign that God was beginning to do what he had promised his People:

> Even if you are exiled to the ends of the world, from there the LORD your God will gather you, and from there he will bring you back.[36]

But not only the Chosen People. Jesus died, "not for the nation only, but to gather into one [all] the dispersed children of God."[37]

The "gift of tongues" at Pentecost foreshadowed what Paul revealed as "the true mystery of God's will," that he "set forth in Christ, as a plan for the fullness of time." It is to "bring all things in the heavens and on earth into one under Christ's headship."[38]

In Christ, at the end of time, all things in heaven and on earth will be "united," "gathered up," "summed up," "recapitulated," "brought together under a single Head." This is Paul's vision of the unification of the human race "in Christ" that the gift of the Holy Spirit at Pentecost foreshadowed and began.

PRAYER FOR UNITY

Perhaps the most striking manifestation of the "gift of the Spirit" is the visible unity that exists among those who have received the life of God by Baptism.[39]

---

[36]*Deuteronomy* 30:4.

[37]*John* 11:52. See also *Thessalonians* 2:1.

[38]*Ephesians* 1:10. This is the *NAB* (1970) version. The *Jerome Biblical Commentary* (1958) translates this as "to unite all things in Christ under one head," and explains: "The verb anekephalaiosasthai literally means to place at the top of a column the sum of figures that have been added." Other efforts at translation are: to "sum up all things in Christ" (*NAB*, 1986); to "unite all things in him" (*RSV*, 1946); to "gather up all things in him" (*New Revised Standard Version*, 1989); "recapitulare omnia in Christo" (Nova Vulgata); "instaurare omnia in Christo" (Vulgate); to "bring everything together under a single head" (ramener toutes choses sous un seul Chef, *New Jerusalem Bible*, 1973). J.B. Phillips, *The New Testament in Modern English*, 1958, translates the thought more freely: "that all human history shall be consummated in Christ, that everything that exists in heaven or earth shall find its perfection and fulfillment in him."

[39]We must never forget that the Church recognizes as reborn through grace all who have been baptized by water, blood, or desire. "By water" refers to sacramental Baptism. "By blood" refers to those who, while preparing for Baptism as catechumens, were (or are) martyred for their faith. "Baptism of desire" refers to all those who, like the Magi, give a response of unconditional faith to the grace God offers them through some sign.

This is what Jesus prayed for at the Last Supper. He asked the Father to give his Church the unity that would make visible the outpouring of his Spirit on earth:

> I ask not only on behalf of these, but also on behalf of those who will believe in me through their word, that they may all be one. As you, Father, are in me and I am in you, may they also be in us, so that the world may believe that you have sent me.
>
> The glory that you have given me I have given them, so that they may be one, as we are one, I in them and you in me, that they may become completely one, so that the world may know that you have sent me and have loved them even as you have loved me.[40]

This is also the prayer of the Church in every Mass.

Before the congregation, through the presiding priest, asks God to make present the once-and-for-all event of Christ offering himself on the cross, the assembly "calls down" the Holy Spirit upon the bread and wine. In this prayer, the Church prays to the Father, "Let your holy Spirit come upon these gifts . . . so that they may become for us the body and blood of our Lord, Jesus Christ."

Then the presider repeats the words of Jesus at the Last Supper, "This is my body . . . the cup of my blood," and lifts up the Body and Blood in the first "elevation."

After this peak moment of the Eucharistic Prayer, there is a second calling down of the Holy Spirit—not on the bread and wine this time, but on the Church herself. The prayer is that the Spirit will unify the Church:

> May all of us who share in the body and blood of Christ be brought together in unity by the Holy Spirit.
>
> May we be filled with his Holy Spirit and become one body, one spirit in Christ.
>
> By your Holy Spirit gather all who share this one bread and one cup into the one body of Christ, a living sacrifice of praise.
>
> The Spirit of Christ is the Spirit of unity. In our desire for unity with all of God's children we experience ourselves as Christ's living body on earth, enriched by his gift of the Holy Spirit.
>
> And that we might live no longer for ourselves but for him, he sent the Holy Spirit from you, Father, as his first gift to those who believe, to complete his work on earth and bring us the fullness of grace.[41]

---

[40]*John* 17:17-23.
[41]Eucharistic Prayer IV.

Christ's work is not complete until all the redeemed have been gathered together into "one flock" with "one shepherd" in the "peace and unity of his kingdom." To long for this is to experience the gift and "groaning" of the Holy Spirit in our hearts.[42]

BEYOND LAW TO SPIRIT

A fourth way to experience the gift of the Spirit is to go beyond law observance to a religion based on response to the Holy Spirit. This is another experience of freedom that is a major theme in the writings of St. Paul.

Paul speaks of a double slavery: slavery to sin and slavery to the law.[43]

The modern word for slavery to the law is legalism. The Gospel word for it is Phariseeism. The Pharisees were not by definition hypocrites, but the members of a Jewish reform party whose goal was to call Israel back to faithful observance of God's law. This was good. Phariseeism degenerated, however, into a mind-set that focused more on law observance than on knowing and loving God. In some it degenerated further into a narrow fixation on the letter of the law rather than on its spirit. These were the ones that Jesus called hypocrites.

Unfortunately, in the generation that preceded the Second Vatican Council, most Catholics were inadvertently, and in varying degrees, formed as unconscious Pharisees. Religion was taught in a way that emphasized keeping commandments and rules more than on seeking a personal relationship with God in knowledge and love. To be good was to avoid sin by obeying the Commandments. We saw no difference between being good and being a good Christian.

This was a long way from the teaching of the Eastern Church fathers cited by the Australian Trappist, Fr. Michael Casey, that "Christian life consists not so much in being good as in becoming God."[44]

To make things even worse, we were not encouraged to grow into deep personal understanding of the reason for the moral laws we kept,

---

[42]See *John* 10:16; *Romans* 8:19 to 9:3.
[43]See *Galatians* 1:4; 2:11-16; 3:23 to 4:10; 4:21 to 5:1; *Romans* 5:12 to 7:25.
[44]Michael Casey, OCSO, *Fully Human, Fully Divine—An Interactive Christololgy*—Liguori/Triumph, 2004, pages vii-ix.

much less for Church rules. We were not directed toward learning the mind of God or the "mind of the Church." We were just taught to do what we were told.

And we did. Blindly, without asking what the goal or purpose of the law was. Women wore hats to Church because that was the rule. If one forgot her hat, she would put a rumpled handkerchief on her head. One hatless and hapless girl, in a story too true to life to be apocryphal, became a legend by holding her hand on top of her head all during Mass! It never occurred to anyone to see this rule as nothing but a dress code, and not a very important one at that.

We were told to fast before Communion. If we had asked ourselves what the purpose of the rule was, we would have recognized immediately that it was to increase our devotion and so make our reception of Communion more beneficial. But we didn't ask. So if we forgot to fast, we automatically abstained from Communion, with the result that we got no benefit from it at all. This was obviously not the intent of the rule, but it wasn't obvious to us because we just obeyed without asking why. (We also never noticed that the law said nothing about abstaining from Communion as a penalty for not fasting. We just assumed, wrongly, that this practice was prescribed as a condition for receiving the Eucharist, not as an enhancement).

We were taught to "go to Mass on Sunday." And we did just that. We went. We were not taught how to participate in the celebration, much less "fully, consciously, and actively" as the Church is urging us to do today. The obligation was to "be there," with our bodies in the pews, whether or not we sat together with others, sang the hymns, understood the ceremony, or offered ourselves consciously and personally with Jesus on the cross for the life of the world.[45]

We went to Mass because it was the law of the Church. But we did not read the Bible, because it wasn't required by law. We did not ask ourselves whether there might be an obligation, attendant on the very nature of Christianity itself, to read the word of God! This was legalism.

---

[45]Vatican II, *Sacred Liturgy / Sacrosanctum Concilium* #14. Quoted in the *General Instruction for the Roman Missal*, July, 2000, no. 18.

In those days Saint Paul in heaven was tearing his hair out. He may still be tearing his hair out today, if he has any left![46]

When Paul insisted that we "must no longer live as the Gentiles live," he meant more than rejecting explicit idolatry. He was saying that we have to go beyond the whole concept of human morality, and specifically human morality as defined by laws and customs, religious or otherwise.

For "Gentiles," read "American culture," or any other planetary culture, including "Catholic culture." It is not only the sins of our society that we must reject; it is the whole world-view: the goals, attitudes, values, customs, life-style, preoccupations, and priorities that are taken for granted in every human society. We must no longer live as "cultural Americans" live, no matter how "nice" they are. Nor is it enough to live as "cultural Catholics."[47] To live as a Christian is to live as Christ. And this we can only do by the gift and power of his Spirit.

Paul insisted over and over again, with an emphasis that brought him to the border of obscenity,[48] that to live as a Christian is to live, not by a set of rules, but in the mystical experience of a life empowered by the Holy Spirit. For Christians, to be "righteous" or "saved" or authentic means to live by the divine light of faith—a living light that cannot be frozen in rules—an outlook we can have only by sharing in the life of God by grace.

> For by grace you have been saved through faith, and this is not your own doing; it is the gift of God, not the result of works, so that no one may boast.[49]

If our focus is on keeping rules that are clearly spelled out in human terms, and which we can faithfully observe through sufficient discipline and will-power, then our religion is a human exercise of performing human acts by human power. And it is a purely human

---

[46]We cannot emphasize enough the seriousness of the "legalist threat" to the Church. Thanks to an intervention by Bishop De Smedt of Bruges, legalism was recognized at the outset of the Second Vatican Council as one of the three ruling attitudes in the Church that must be reformed. Bishop De Smedt pointed out that the agenda originally drawn up by Curia officials in the Vatican was characterized by three things: legalism, clericalism, and triumphalism. The bishops rejected these three approaches as destructive and drew up a new agenda. These three attitudes strike respectively at the heart of our baptismal consecration as prophets, priests, and kings or stewards of the kingship of Christ.

[47]For a more extensive treatment of this, see my book *His Way*, where "cultural Catholicism" is also referred to as "civil religion."

[48]*Galatians* 5:1-12.

[49]*Ephesians* 2:8-9.

experience. It is a good life of upright behavior that does not depend on any experience of the Holy Spirit.

This is what many younger people today, who have turned away from the Church, call "religion" as opposed to "spirituality."[50]

This is the religion of the Pharisees. It is the religion Paul grew up in, fought for with fanatical zeal while he was persecuting the Christians, and then, after his conversion, fought against for the rest of his apostolic life.[51]

When we arrive at the stage where we consciously seek to be guided, not just by formulated rules, but by the light of the Holy Spirit enlightening us in prayer, and by his unpredictable inspirations nudging us into the unforeseen from day to day, we have opened ourselves to the experience of the Spirit.[52]

Then we find ourselves getting insights into demands of the Gospel that go far beyond what the "rules" require. We find ourselves moved to do things we don't "have to" do. We do them because we think God wants us to do them. We begin to live out our faith in ways that are new and different from what "everyone" does. And we no longer accept to do some of the things that "everyone" accepts as perfectly compatible with Christianity. In short, we become "prophets" living lives of prophetic witness.

Now we live by Paul's baptismal exhortation in which he not only warns, "Do not be conformed to this world," but positively urges, "Be transformed by the renewing of your minds." He wants our thinking to be so transformed that we will be able to "discern what is the will of

---

[50]One of the problems emerging in the twenty-to-forty-year-olds of "Generation X" is the perceived distinction between "religion" and "spirituality." A deacon in campus ministry observed, "The students want spirituality, but they don't think they will find it in religion." The Australian David Ranson begins his book *Across the Great Divide: Bridging Spirituality and Religion Today* with a quote from psychologist Kenneth Pargament: "Whether we welcome it or lament it, there is now, at least in popular consciousness, an undeniable split between 'religion' and 'spirituality.' People have no difficulty in claiming themselves to be 'spiritual' or to be on a 'spiritual journey' . . . [while] they disavow themselves of being 'religious' . . . Religion is now thought of as the organizational, the ritual, the ideological, while spirituality is associated with the personal, the affective, the experiential, and the thoughtful. As a result, a person can be spiritual without being religious, and religious without being spiritual." (Ranson is published by St. Paul's Publications, Strathfield, New South Wales, 2002. See page 9).
[51]See *Acts* 22:3-8.
[52]Compare this to what St. Teresa of Avila says about the difference between those in the third and fourth "dwelling places" in her *Interior Castle*.

God"—not just what is "good," but what is "acceptable" for those called to live as the body of Christ on earth, and even what is "perfect."[53]

To experience this transformation is to experience the gift of the Holy Spirit.

CHANGING THE MORAL QUESTION

One simple way to do "all of the above" and grow into the abiding experience of the Holy Spirit, is to change our standard of morality. We decide never to ask again just whether something is right or wrong, but always to ask, "How will this bear witness to the values of Jesus?"

We don't have to be so saintly that we will always do what bears witness to Christ and his values. To pledge that would be unrealistic and ultimately discouraging. We just have to develop the habit of always asking the question.

To form that habit is a further step toward fulfilling our side of the baptismal covenant. If we accept, by Baptism, God's promise to give us the gift of the Holy Spirit, we implicitly promise on our part to live by the Spirit he gives.

If we do this, little by little everything in our life will change. Almost painlessly.

And we will experience ourselves as living by the gift of the Holy Spirit.

A SIMPLE SUGGESTION: CONTINUAL CONVERSION

A simple, easy way to experience the gift of the Holy Spirit—simple but not simplistic—is to promise God we will keep making constant changes in our lifestyle.

In the *Rule* of Saint Benedict, which has set the standard for monastic life in the western hemisphere for almost fifteen hundred years, a principal vow is conversatio morum. The monks promise "continual conversion of life." This is an element of Benedictine spirituality that secular Christians, Christians "in the world," can appropriate, because

---

[53]*Romans* 12:1-2.

it is already implicit in the acceptance we give to our baptismal consecration as prophets.

To make this promise of "continual conversion" explicit is a practical way to fulfill our commitment to be "prophets." It also ensures that we will experience the gift of the Holy Spirit. What does this mean in practice?

It means we simply promise God that we will keep making changes in our lifestyle. Changes in the way we eat, drink, drive, dress, speak, spend our time, spend our money. Changes in the books on our shelves, the pictures on our walls, the expressions on our faces, the programs we watch on TV, the things we dream about in our idle moments. Any change will do, so long as it is guided by a desire to make more and more elements of our lifestyle bear witness to the values of Jesus Christ.

We don't promise big changes or small ones; just changes. We don't promise to make a fixed number of changes in a given period of time. We just promise to "keep making" changes. And we don't promise to make all the changes we may think God wants us to make. To bind ourselves too specifically is unrealistic. And burdensome. If we did, we would not be able to live up to it. We would get discouraged. And give up.

We just promise to "keep making continual changes in our lifestyle." We don't specify the promise any more than that. But we take our commitment very seriously. Because we hold back from making this commitment something hard and demanding, we have no excuse for not keeping it. If we aren't up to making hard changes, we are committed to make easy ones.

All we promise is forward motion.

Sailors have a term called "steerage way." It means a ship is moving just fast enough for the rudder to work. There is enough pressure of water against the blade of the rudder to modify the course of the ship. That is what this promise is: to keep moving forward just enough to have "steerage way": enough so that a little pressure from the Holy Spirit can influence our direction. And influence our direction the Spirit will!

To be realistic, of course, we have to establish some checkpoints. If we just commit ourselves once and for all, we will soon forget about it. So we need to ask ourselves periodically, "Have I made any changes in my life this week? Or this month?" We can remember to ask the question by associating it with something we know we are going to do anyway—like paying our utility bill. Or we can do it every Sunday on our way to church. Or during the collection. For Catholics, a good time would be during the Presentation of Gifts at Mass. When the bread and wine are brought forward—with the collection—we can ask what changes we are sending up to be placed on the altar with them.

The important thing is to keep asking the question—as in the previous suggestion—and to keep making enough changes to keep up "forward motion." Then we will experience the wind of the Holy Spirit in our sails and God's hand on the tiller.

And we will know that Jesus has kept his promise:

"You will receive power when the Holy Spirit has come upon you; and you will be my witnesses . . . to the ends of the earth."[54]

KEY POINTS:

- Baptism gives a new meaning and purpose to our lives. We receive the "messianic anointing" by which we are empowered, consecrated, and commissioned to carry on the mission of Jesus Prophet, Priest, and King.

- To be a "prophet" means to "profess" the faith in such a way that we bear witness to the Good News. This profession, to be effective, must be above all a profession in action rather than in words. This witness is the key to "evangelization."

- The only way the world will be evangelized is through the witness of Christian lives that make the reality of Christ's resurrection visible. Lives resplendent in faith, hope, and love; lives that can only be explained by the work of the Spirit of Jesus Christ risen, alive, and active in those who believe.

- To bear witness to Christ, our lifestyle must radiate faith in values that go beyond anything perceived, understood, or hoped for in

---

[54]*Acts* 1:8; and see 8:15, 19; 19:2; *Galatians* 3:2.

this world. It must raise questions that can only be answered through divine faith, hope, and love.

- We don't carry on this mission alone. We continue it with Jesus. We are co-missioned with him and empowered by the gift of the Holy Spirit.

- This witness is in a special way the call and commitment of the laity because they live in the world, in the "ordinary circumstances" of family and social life. Everywhere they are, everything they do, should express and reveal the faith-vision in their hearts.

- The "gift of the Spirit" is given with Baptism. This was a visible experience in the early Church and still is today.

- The first way to experience the gift of the Spirit is to make a conscious break with the idolatry of our culture.

- A second way of experiencing the gift of the Spirit is to realize we have become so "different" from others in outlook and self-expression that we no longer "speak the same language." Because we no longer see the world or respond to it the way others do, we acquire a certain "immunity" to the influence of the culture.

- A third way to experience the gift of the Spirit is to get into contact with an inner drive impelling us to desire unity with all people. This is the deeper meaning of the "gift of tongues" that was experienced at Pentecost.

- A fourth way to experience the gift of the Spirit is to go beyond legalism to a religion based on response to the Holy Spirit. This takes us beyond what many younger people today, who have turned away from the Church, call "religion" as opposed to "spirituality."

QUESTIONS FOR REFLECTION AND DISCUSSION:

- How have you experienced the "gift of the Holy Spirit"?

- This booklet explains four ways of experiencing the Spirit. How many of them have you experienced, and how?

- Have you experienced a new meaning and purpose to your life because of your "messianic anointing" to carry on the mission of Jesus?

- Do you have an awareness of being "co-missioned" to work with Jesus, empowered by the gift of his Holy Spirit?

- Does your lifestyle raise questions in people's minds that can only be answered through an explanation of the Good News?

A SUGGESTED KEY DECISION:

A simple, easy way to experience the gift of the Holy Spirit—simple but not simplistic— is to promise God we will keep making constant changes in our lifestyle. This is guided by the goal of—little by little— making everything we do bear witness to the values of Jesus.

Decide never to ask again just whether something is right or wrong, but always to ask, "How will this bear witness to the values of Jesus?"

The Fourth Promise of Baptism
Posterity

*"I am the vine, you are the branches.
Those who abide in me and I in them bear much fruit."*

*"My little children... I am again in the pain of childbirth
until Christ is formed in you."*

*"As Christ was anointed Priest...
so may you live always as a member of his body."*[1]

In this chapter we ask a question that remains a surprise for many: "Are you aware that you are a priest? Do you know that you became a priest at Baptism?"

What does that mean? What mystery is enfolded in it? What promise does it hold out to you? To what are you consciously committed by it?

This chapter will take you into the mystical dimension of ministry. It will explain what the word "ministry" adds to the meaning of "mission." The purpose of this is just to show you how, by living out your baptismal consecration to share in the mission of Jesus as Prophet, Priest, and King, you will be led progressively into greater union with Christ. It is a union in mind and will and heart, so that Saint Paul's prayer (and Jesus' desire) will be realized in you:

> I pray that you may have the power to comprehend, with all the saints, what is the breadth and length and height and depth, and to know the love of Christ that surpasses knowledge, so that you may be filled with all the fullness of God.[2]

It belongs to human nature to want our lives to count for something. We do not want to die leaving nothing behind us: no accomplishments, no descendants, no memories, no sign of our ever having existed on earth. Even though we know we will live forever in heaven, we still want to leave something behind us that prolongs our presence in this world.

---

[1]*John* 15:5; *Rite of Baptism for Children*, no. 98.
[2]See *Ephesians* 3:18-21.

God answered this desire throughout Scripture with repeated promises of a "posterity"—through progeny, offspring, descendants.

The prime example was Abraham. God had blessed him with possessions: he was "very rich in livestock, in silver, and in gold." But he complained to the Lord that he was childless: "You have given me no offspring, and so a slave born in my house is to be my heir." Abraham's name would cease to exist on earth. All of his possessions—all traces of his existence—would be divided up among others. So God promised Abraham a posterity:

> "I will indeed bless you, and I will make your offspring as numerous as the stars of heaven and as the sand that is on the seashore."[3]

We know that this promise was fulfilled literally in the mystery of Jesus Christ, "Son of David, son of Abraham." "In Christ" the whole of redeemed humanity, every nation, tribe, and person, will be "gathered up," joined together and united in one body, to form that "perfect man who is Christ come to full stature." This is the mystery of the "end time," and the purpose and goal of all creation.[4]

Throughout Scripture, the blessing God promised to his chosen ones, and to all who lived by his word, was a posterity. This was his promise to Abraham, Isaac, Jacob, David, and to the "Suffering Servant" who was Jesus himself ("he shall see his offspring, and shall prolong his days").[5]

Fruitfulness was promised to all God's faithful people:

> "If you will only obey the LORD your God . . . blessed shall be the fruit of your womb, the fruit of your ground, and the fruit of your livestock . . . and the LORD will . . . bless all your undertakings." "Happy is everyone who fears the LORD, who walks in his ways. You shall eat the fruit of the labor of your hand. . . . Your wife will be like a fruitful vine within your house; your children will be like olive shoots around your table. . . . May you see your children's children."[6]

---

[3]*Genesis* 13:2; 15:2-5; 22:17.
[4]*Matthew* 1:1; *Colossians* 1:15-19; *Ephesians* 1:1-23; 4:11.
[5]*Genesis* 26:4; 35:11; *1 Chronicles* 17:11; *Jeremiah* 33:22; *Isaiah* 53:10. See also Sarah, the mother of Isaac (*Genesis* 17:15-19); Rebekah, the mother of Jacob (*Genesis* 25:21); Rachel, the mother of Jacob's sons Joseph and Benjamin (*Genesis* 29:31; 30:22-24, 34); Hannah, the mother of Samuel (*1 Samuel* 1:2-20); and Elizabeth, the mother of John the Baptizer (*Luke* 1:7-13). All of these women were barren, but by God's special intervention, all conceived sons who had a special role to play in the history of salvation.
[6]*Deuteronomy* 28:1-18; *Isaiah* 14:22; *Psalm* 128.

This promise reached its climax in Elizabeth's words to Mary, "Blessed are you among women, and blessed is the fruit of your womb!" The apostle Paul saw this same fruitfulness as the goal and result of all his ministry: "My little children, for whom I am again in the pain of childbirth until Christ is formed in you. . . . . I became your father through the gospel." The apostle John declared he had "no greater joy than this, to hear that my children are walking in the truth."[7]

The promise made to Mary—"Blessed is the fruit of thy womb"— is the promise God makes to every person baptized into his life and ministry: "Blessed is the fruit of your life." Our lives will bear fruit, a fruit that will last forever, because the "fruit of our lives" will be Christ himself, brought to birth and nurtured by us to "full stature" in ourselves and in one another. This is the mystery of Christian life and ministry: to be "in the pain of childbirth until Christ is formed" in ourselves and in all to whom we minister.

MEDIATING THE LIFE OF GOD

The essence of Christian ministry is the mystery of mediating the divine life of God to one another.

At Baptism, we "presented our bodies as a living sacrifice to God," so that, wherever our live bodies are, we would be "sacrificed" to doing the will and work of Christ living within us.[8]

Jesus told us what that work is: "I came that they might have life, life to the full." The "grace of our Lord Jesus Christ" is the favor of sharing in the divine life of God. The goal of Christian ministry is to communicate that divine life to others.[9]

By grace, God's divine life is in us, but invisible, enclosed within our bodies. It only becomes profitable to others when we share it by giving expression to it in our flesh, through physical words and actions. When we do this, we are allowing our bodies to become the medium for Christ's own self-expression.

Just as grace is "the favor of sharing in God's own divine life," the actions proper to grace are actions in which the divine action of God living within us "takes flesh" in our human activities.

---

[7]*Luke* 1:42; *Galatians* 4:19; *1 Corinthians* 4:14-15; *Ephesians* 4:7-16; *3 John* 1:4.
[8]*Romans* 12:1.
[9]*John* 10:10.

Those activities are essentially acts of divine faith, hope, and love. To give physical expression to graced faith, hope, or love is to let God express visibly and physically in our human actions his divine truth, his divine promises, his divine love. The essence and mystery of Christian ministry is simply grace expressed.

For example: faith is the mystery of sharing in God's own act of knowing. God cannot empower any creature to know what he knows as he knows it. That is proper to God alone. Jesus said this clearly: "No one knows the Son except the Father, and no one knows the Father except the Son." It is impossible for any creature to know God as God. So when Jesus added "and anyone to whom the Son chooses to reveal him," this could only mean that he was going to reveal the Father to us by letting us share in his own divine act of knowing the Father. No one can know the Father except the Son—and those who by the grace of sharing in the Son's own divine life have become filii in Filio, "sons and daughters in the Son." We know the Father by being "in Christ," sharing in his own act of knowing. This is the gift and mystery of faith.[10]

And so, when we express our faith in physical words and actions, Jesus within us is expressing in and through our bodies—which by Baptism have become his body—the divine truth which he himself sees and knows as God. In our graced words, the words of Jesus himself "take flesh." Our bodies become the medium for God's own self-expression. In our human words, the inexpressible, divine truth of God within us is expressed and communicated to others. Through our graced self-expression, we "mediate" to others God's gift, God's expression of divine truth.

The same is true of love. God in our hearts is loving with infinite, divine love every person we deal with. But this does not do any good to someone who is totally unaware of it. So we "mediate" the love of God to others by giving expression to it, in and through our bodies. When we express graced love for others in word and action, Jesus within us is giving expression to his own divine love. He heals, comforts, and draws people to himself by acting in us and through us who are his living body on earth.

---

[10]*Matthew* 11:27.

The essence of ministry is expression. Self-expression. The expression of our graced self through the making-visible of our faith, our hope, our love, which are God's divine life within us.

This is what it means to say that the mystery of Christian ministry is to "mediate the divine life of God to one another."

This is a mystery of fruitfulness. It is the application to us all of Elizabeth's words to Mary: "Blessed is the fruit of your womb"—blessed is the fruit of our lives. It is the fulfillment of Jesus' promise at the Last Supper:

> "You did not choose me but I chose you. And I appointed you to go and bear fruit, fruit that will last."
>
> Every branch that bears fruit [my Father] prunes to make it bear more fruit. . . .
>
> Abide in me as I abide in you. Just as the branch cannot bear fruit by itself unless it abides in the vine, neither can you unless you abide in me. . . .
>
> I am the vine, you are the branches. Those who abide in me and I in them bear much fruit, because apart from me you can do nothing. . . .
>
> My Father is glorified by this, that you bear much fruit and become my disciples.[11]

The fourth promise of Baptism is fruitful ministry: the blessing of an everlasting posterity. This is the promise contained in our baptismal consecration as priests.

WE ARE "PRIESTS IN THE PRIEST"

It is the teaching of the Church, taken straight from the *Letter to the Hebrews*, that there is only one Priest: Jesus Christ.[12]

We also profess that there is only one Son of God: Jesus, the "only Son of the Father." But all who have been baptized into Christ are true "sons and daughters in the Son." In the same way, there is only one true Priest, Jesus; but all who are "in Christ" by Baptism are "priests in the Priest." Every baptized Christian is a priest.

---

[11]*John* 15:2-16.
[12]See *Hebrews* 8:13 to 10:23. In the New Testament no Christian is called a priest except Jesus himself in the *Letter to the Hebrews*. However, the first *Letter of Peter* includes all the baptized in his "holy" and "royal priesthood" (*1 Peter* 2:5-9). On this see Donald Gelpi, S.J., "Priesthood," in *The New Dictionary of Sacramental Worship*, ed. Peter Fink (Liturgical Press, 1990).

Over the centuries, an unfortunate lack of attention to terminology has distorted our Catholic understanding of priesthood. We use the word "priest" in ordinary conversation to designate the ordained clergy. But in fact, the English word "priest" comes from the Greek word *presbyteros*, meaning "elder" (from which came the French *prêtre*, the German Priester, and the English priest). When we call someone a "priest" today, what we really mean is what the New Testament calls a "presbyter." If we use the word "priest" correctly, we will understand that it belongs properly to Jesus alone, and by extension to all who are "priests in the Priest" by Baptism. The ordained priests are "presbyters," who, in addition to Baptism, became priests in a different way by being ordained to special functions of priesthood through the sacrament of Holy Orders.[13]

This moves us to ask, "What functions were we committed and empowered to perform by our baptismal consecration as priests?"

MINISTRY AND SACRIFICE

The two functions that the word "priest" immediately calls to mind are "ministry" and "sacrifice." These are associated with priesthood as such. And in reality they are one and the same. To sacrifice our time in ministry is to sacrifice our life.

On this earth, "life" and "time" are co-terminous: they begin and end together. So to give to another a moment, or an hour of our time in ministry, is to sacrifice a moment or hour of our life. Jesus said there is no greater love than this: to lay down one's life—or, we might add, any part of one's life—for a friend. To make the ministering, life-mediating expression of faith, hope, and love our constant intention all day long is to "lay down our life" constantly in love.[14]

---

[13]See Patrick J. Dunn, Bishop of Auckland, New Zealand: *Priesthood: A Re-Examination of the Roman Catholic Theology of the Presbyterate*: Alba House, New York, 1990, p. 110. Bishop Dunn points out that in the Second Vatican Council the bishops tried to restore a more authentic understanding of the relationship between clergy and laity by "avoiding terms such as 'clergy' and 'priest,'" and by returning to the New Testament expression "presbyter" with its collegial and fraternal associations. . . . As a general rule the conciliar texts try to follow the Scriptures and to restrict the word "priest" (sacerdos) to Jesus himself and to the "common priesthood" of the baptized; and when talking about the ordained they use the word "presbyteros." But the English translation uncritically translates both "sacerdos" and "presbyteros" as "priest."
[14]*John* 15:13.

To minister to another as priest is to sacrifice oneself for another as victim. They go together; especially since the Victim Jesus offered as Priest was his own body. We, then, who by being the body of Christ are "priests in the Priest," are by definition also "victims in the Victim." We give life to others as Jesus did: by dying. Every act of ministry is an act of "dying to self." Every time we use our bodies to express faith, hope, or love to another, we are giving our "flesh for the life of the world." We do it through self-expression.[15]

"Dying" Through Self-Expression

Self-expression—if the "self" we are expressing is our graced self—is by nature an act of dying to self. It is self-gift. It is vulnerability. It is giving our "flesh for the life of the world" by surrendering our bodies to be the medium of Christ's own life-giving self-expression.

We "die to ourselves" in vulnerability when we express our thoughts about religion, or our feelings about Jesus, or share with someone an experience of God that we think we might have had. We make ourselves vulnerable when we pray together with others; or when we show our devotion—appropriately, of course—in public.

All ministry is "dying to self" in service. We "die to ourselves" when we open the door for another, replenish someone's drink, or tell a problem-maker in a gentle, caring way a truth that needs to be told. We mediate Christ's love whenever we reach out to others or invite others into our life, our circle of friends, our community of faith, or when we bring people to Mass.

We "die to ourselves" when we don't feel like singing at Mass but sing anyway—to express the graced, but unfelt, enthusiasm the Spirit within us brings to the celebration. This is ministry and sacrifice.

We "die to ourselves" when we show appreciation for another, especially when we are hesitant to do so; for example, because it is someone we don't know very well. If we take the risk and do it, we are letting Christ express his appreciation through us. This is the ministry of self-expression.

---

[15] *John* 6:51.

We can minister by showing love with no personal interaction at all: planting flowers in our front yard to brighten up the neighborhood; putting up Christmas decorations outdoors to share the Good News; picking up a piece of paper on the floor or a beer can on the sidewalk; wearing a medal or a cross to quietly introduce the dimension of the sacred where we work; putting a bowl of candy on our desk in invitation.

Ministry is dying to self because ministry is living for others. There is no greater gift.

Jesus came that we might "have life and have it to the full."[16] To give us life, he died. Our baptismal consecration as priests commits us to "die to ourselves" in order to live totally for God and other people in love. We do this by saying to the whole human race, in union with Christ on the cross, "This is my body given up for you."

What transforms our service to others into ministry is love—and specifically love expressed in our bodies as an expression of the divine love of Christ actively loving within us. To love is to heal, to give life. To let Christ love through all our bodily words and actions is to give our "flesh for the life of the world." This is to live out our Baptismal consecration as priests.

Paul wrote: "For to me, living is Christ and dying is gain. If I am to live in the flesh, that means fruitful labor for me." Priesthood, by its very nature, is dying to self by living in such a way that we use our flesh to give life to others in fruitful ministry.

PRIESTHOOD IS PROCREATIVE

This makes priesthood procreative by nature. Our baptismal consecration as priests carries with it the promise of an eternal posterity. We live to bring Christ to birth and to maturity in every person we encounter.

Christian tradition has seen the open side of Christ on the cross as a womb from which the Church was born. In this image, the life-giving love of Christ's sacrifice as Priest and Victim, and the fecundity of priesthood, are affirmed as one.

---

[16]*John* 10:10.

Ministry Is Union

Through Baptism we share in the life—and in the priesthood—of Jesus, as branches share in the life and fruitfulness of the vine.

When Jesus said, "I am the vine, you are the branches. Those who abide in me and I in them bear much fruit," this was a double promise: the promise of union with himself, and of the fruitfulness in ministry that flows from that union.[17]

For the sake of clarity, we are going to make a distinction here between mission and ministry. Ministry is part of our mission, of course. But when we speak of "mission," it suggests the clarion call of great deeds to accomplish, the power of prophetic witness, the privilege of being "co-workers" with Jesus in establishing the kingdom of God on earth.[18] In "mission," we are being "sent."

When we speak of "ministry," however, the flavor of the word is more of gentle, nurturing care; personal life-enhancement and healing. "Ministry" is to groups as well as to individuals, of course; but, it is also readily pictured as one-on-one ministration, while we don't usually think of having a "mission" to one person.

"Ministry" is almost synonymous with "love."

Also, where "mission" could seem to focus on an objective, even impersonal "result" to be achieved (for example, the "Kingdom of God"), "ministry" is subjective, a caring for people. "Mission" could be driven by desire for accomplishment; "ministry" can only be driven by love.

In the Last Supper discourse, Jesus says "Abide in me." In this text, ministry appears as something we do in living union with Jesus, in closeness with him.

We are not trying to make a complete separation here between mission—which we have associated especially with "prophetic witness"—and ministry, which we are associating here with our consecration as

---

[17]See *John* 15:1-16.
[18]See *1 Corinthians* 3:9: we are co-workers with God (synergoi), quoted in Vatican II on "Missionary Activity," no. 15 and *2 Corinthians* 6:1: co-working (synergountes). No one has expressed this call better than St. Ignatius of Loyola in the key "Kingdom" meditation of his *Spiritual Exercises*, nos. 91-98.

priests. The first element of our mission is to bear witness to Jesus Christ as prophets, and specifically to Jesus risen from the dead and living in us. But this witness obviously depends on union with Christ. Our lives bear witness to the resurrection in the measure that our lifestyle, our behavior, our "love, joy, and peace," even in the midst of adversity, cannot be explained except by the presence and power of his risen life in us. In the same way, we can have no authentic ministry as "priests" unless our lifestyle as "prophets" bears witness to the gift of the Spirit within us.

The difference between mission and ministry, as we are dealing with them here, is simply one of emphasis and focus. As we look deeper, we see it also as a difference in the way we experience the fulfillment of Baptism's promises.

Union Through Surrender

We have associated "mission" with our baptismal consecration as prophets and the promise of the "gift of the Spirit" empowering us to bear witness. "You will receive power when the Holy Spirit has come upon you; and you will be my witnesses in Jerusalem, in all Judea and Samaria, and to the ends of the earth."[19] In witness, the emphasis is on "with-ness." We stand with Jesus in bearing witness to his truth, his values. The Holy Spirit is with us, guiding and empowering us. We are "sent out," but Jesus is still with us, and especially by the gift of his Spirit.

In ministry, the emphasis is on "within-ness."

> I will ask the Father, and he will give you another Advocate, to be with you forever. . . . You know him, because he abides with you, and he will be in you. . . . On that day you will know that I am in my Father, and you in me, and I in you. . . . Those who love me will keep my word, and my Father will love them, and we will come to them and make our home with them. . . .[20]

This "within-ness" is an experience of love: God coming to us in love, God abiding within us in love, God expressing himself through us in love.

In mission, the emphasis is more on what we are trying to do, what we are proclaiming, what values we are embodying, what we are trying

---

[19] *Acts* 1:8.
[20] *John* 14:15-23.

to accomplish. In ministry, the focus is more on who we are, who is present within us, who is expressing himself through us. Ministry is an experience of the person of Jesus within us, communicating his divine life through us to the persons to whom we minister.

For these reasons, we associate "mission" with the "power" of the Holy Spirit. But ministry is simply surrender. It is letting Christ within us, through his gentle, loving Spirit within us, express himself in and through our human actions.

The promise of ministry is that the Father, Son, and Spirit will "abide" in us, and that if we abide in them, and enter deeply into union with them through surrender, we will bear fruit like branches whose life is that of the vine.

> Abide in me as I abide in you. . . . I am the vine, you are the branches. Those who abide in me and I in them bear much fruit, because apart from me you can do nothing. . . . If you abide in me, and my words abide in you, ask for whatever you wish, and it will be done for you. My Father is glorified by this, that you bear much fruit. . . . As the Father has loved me, so I have loved you; abide in my love. If you keep my commandments, you will abide in my love. . . .[21]

In consecrating us to ministry, what Jesus promised us is abiding union with himself, the Father, and the Spirit. Union with him who is the Life. United to him, we receive Life and we give Life. Life flowing to us and through us who are living branches on the vine of Life.

Love is the greatest power on earth. But when we let God express love through us, we do not experience it as power. We experience it as surrender.

Surrender is the key to ministry. We don't think of letting Christ express his love through us as an accomplishment. It is indeed something we do through the power of the Holy Spirit, but we don't experience it as power. We experience it as surrender.

We surrender ourselves to Jesus living within us; Jesus whose body we are, so that he might give expression, in and through our physical words and actions, to his truth, his promises, his love. We surrender ourselves to Jesus in the same total obedience with which he surren-

---

[21]See *John* 15:4-9.

dered to the Father. He "humbled himself and became obedient to the point of death—even death on a cross." We surrender ourselves in order to "abide" totally in him and in his love. This was his promise:

> If you keep my commandments, you will abide in my love just as I have kept my Father's commandments and abide in his love. . . . This is my commandment, that you love one another as I have loved you. No one has greater love than this, to lay down one's life for one's friends.[22]

Ministry, sacrifice, surrender, union with Christ in life-giving love, they are all the same reality. Through ministry we "make real" our experience of the promise God made to us at Baptism when we "became" Christ the Priest. We also make real our fulfillment of the promise that was implicit in our acceptance of that consecration: the commitment to "abide in him," and bear fruit through union with him:

> Abide in me as I abide in you. . . . I am the vine, you are the branches. Those who abide in me and I in them bear much fruit. . . . As the Father has loved me, so I have loved you; abide in my love.[23]

SPOUSAL LOVE

Through dedication to ministry, we experience the mystery of spousal love with Christ. This is the mystery of Baptism. By Baptism, we become members of the Church which, according to the teaching of Scripture, is the "bride of Christ." So all who are in the Church are "brides in the Bride."

Saint Paul associates this mystery specifically with Baptism:

> Husbands, love your wives, just as Christ loved the church and gave himself up for her, in order to make her holy by cleansing her with the washing of water by the word. . . . In the same way, husbands should love their wives as they do their own bodies . . . just as Christ does for the church, because we are members of his body. . . . This is a great mystery, and I am applying it to Christ and the church.[24]

The love to which we are called is spousal love for God. What does that mean?

---

[22]*Philippians* 2:5-11; *John* 15:10-13. See also *Romans* 5:17-19; 6:16-19; *Hebrews* 5:5-10.
[23]*John* 15:4-9.
[24]*Ephesians* 5:28-32. See *Matthew* 25:1; *John* 3:29; *Revelation* 18:23; 19:7; 21:2, 9; 22:17. If any men are put off by the thought of being a "bride in the Bride," they will just have to get beyond the gender distinction as women have to do when told they are "sons in the Son," "priests in the Priest" and "kings in the King." In some cases we can substitute a word that is not gender specific, but when we cannot, we mustn't let the image block out the mystery.

All love is commitment. A commitment is a free choice that endures. In Scripture, the phrase that constitutes the "virtual definition of God" is "enduring love."[25]

Spousal love is an enduring choice to do those things that foster perfect union of mind and will and heart with another. This is the choice that defines the relationship with Jesus Christ that we entered into by Baptism. The goal of that relationship, and of Christian life itself, is to arrive at the "perfection of love." This is the reality of what St. Teresa of Avila calls the "spiritual marriage." It is the climax of our spiritual journey.[26]

What Baptism promised us, as the fruit of living out this mystery of spousal love, was union with Jesus the Beloved, a union like that of the branches with the vine. A union which, like human marriage, is intended to be fruitful.

> Abide in me as I abide in you. . . . I am the vine, you are the branches. Those who abide in me and I in them bear much fruit . . . My Father is glorified by this, that you bear much fruit. . . .[27]

We live out our union with Christ in ministry. The relationship of spousal love entails a commitment to ministry. "This is the . . . purpose of this spiritual marriage: the birth always of good works." All that Teresa teaches about prayer is intended to foster ministry and service to others: "Let us desire and be occupied in prayer not for the sake of our enjoyment but so as to have the strength to serve."[28]

> Works are what the Lord wants! He desires that if you see a Sister who is sick to whom you can bring some relief, you have compassion on her . . . and that if she is suffering pain, you also feel it; and that, if necessary, you fast so that she might eat . . . because you know it is your Lord's desire. This is true union with his will. . . .[29]

---

[25]See *John* 1:14 in the *New American Bible* (1970); *Exodus* 34:6; *2 Samuel* 2:6; 15:20; *Psalms* 25:10; 61:7; 85:10; 86:15; 89:14; 98:3. The phrase "steadfast love," appears 173 times in the Bible.
[26]See *The Interior Castle*, V, ch. 3, no. 7, where Teresa asks her nuns, "What do you think his will is? . . . That we be completely perfect." This is the teaching of Vatican II: "Thus it is evident to everyone that all the faithful of Christ of whatever rank or status are called to the fullness of the Christian life and to the perfection of love" (*The Church* no. 40, p. 67). See also in Kavanaugh's Introduction to the *Interior Castle*: "The ultimate goal, then, of Teresa's journey, the spiritual marriage, is a union with Christ. . . ." *The Collected Works of St. Teresa of Avila*, Vol. 2, translated by Kieran Kavanaugh, O.C.D., and Otilio Rodrigues, O.C.D., Institute of Carmelite Studies, Washington, D.C., 1980, pages 277-278.
[27]See *John* 15:4-9.
[28]*Interior Castle*, VII, ch. 4, nos. 6 and 12.
[29]*Interior Castle*, V, ch. 3, no. 11.

Teresa makes God's will fairly simple:

The Lord asks of us only two things: love of his Majesty and love of our neighbor. These are what we must work for. By observing them with perfection, we do his will and so will be united with him.

Then she makes it even simpler:

The most certain sign, in my opinion . . . is whether we observe well the love of neighbor. We cannot know whether or not we love God . . . but we can know whether we love our neighbor. And be certain that the more advanced you see you are in love for your neighbor the more advanced you will be in the love of God.

She gets very practical:

"If we practice love of neighbor with great perfection, we will have done everything." This is ministry.[30]

Teresa makes it clear that she is talking about graced love:

"We will not reach perfection in the love of neighbor if that love doesn't rise from love of God at its root." In the same way, ministry is not truly Christian unless it is the expression of its only authentic source: God's own divine love in our hearts. So in arriving at constant, habitual, graced love of neighbor, we experience the deeper mystery of our union with Christ as branches united to the vine. This is the fruit of that loving surrender to God which consists in letting Jesus Christ express himself in and through our human actions. . . .[31]

This is Christian ministry. It is to this ministry that we were committed by our baptismal consecration as priests.

THE WIT PRAYER

The "WIT prayer" as a way of entering into the first promise of Baptism. We propose it again as a way of experiencing the fourth promise: "Those who abide in me, and I in them, bear much fruit."[32]

We pray upon waking, "Lord, I give you my body. Live this day with me, live this day in me, live this day through me." And we add: "Let me think with your thoughts, speak with your words, and act as your

---

[30]*Interior Castle*, V, ch. 3, nos. 7-9.
[31]*Interior Castle*, V, ch. 3, no. 9.
[32]This is very similar to the practices proposed in the two spiritual classics: *The Practice of the Presence of God*, by Br. Lawrence of the Resurrection, O.C.D., and *Self Abandonment to Divine Providence*, by J.P. de Caussade, S.J. All three consist, essentially, in awareness of Christ present within us and adoring surrender to his will.

body on earth." Before everything we do, all day, we continue to pray, "Lord do this with me, do this in me, do this through me." But now the emphasis is less on "with" and more on "in" and "through."

If we form the habit of saying this prayer all through the day, trying habitually and consciously to let Christ express himself in and through our words and actions, we gradually become aware that we are indeed united to him, and he is indeed speaking and acting through us.

"Lord, do this with me, do this in me, do this through me. Let me think with your thoughts, speak with your words, and act as your body on earth."

We are not talking about particular dramatic instances of mystical experience. It is just that we begin to become aware, to know, that often what we say and do does not come just from us. We experience ourselves as "playing above our heads"—saying and doing things that are above our ordinary way of speaking and acting.

And we know that it is Jesus within us who is acting, Jesus who is expressing himself in us and through us.

Then we experience the truth of his promise: "Those who abide in me and I in them bear much fruit."

A SIMPLE SUGGESTION: MAKE EVERY ENCOUNTER LOVE

A simple way to live out our consecration to ministry day by day—simple, but not simplistic—is just to concentrate on being loving to every person we deal with. This means we never allow ourselves to have a purely "professional" or functional interaction with anyone. We always acknowledge in some way, no matter how small, that we recognize the other as a human being like ourselves, with feelings, dreams, disappointments, and desires. Without being explicit about it, we consciously treat every person we deal with, not only as a friend, but as a child of the Father, a brother or sister in Christ.

Suppose you are going through the check-out counter at the supermarket. The lady at the register tells you what you owe. You pay it and leave. You have just implicitly denied the faith!

Suppose the clerk happens to be your sister. And your interaction with her was purely business. Don't you think you would hear about that? "Hey! Hello . . . ? You don't say hello to your sister? You don't say a word to show you recognize who I am? What is the matter with you?"

We must acknowledge the presence of Christ in other people. Just as he acknowledged us. When Jesus was speaking to the crowds and someone told him, "Look, your mother and your brothers are standing outside, wanting to speak to you," he replied:

> "Who is my mother, and who are my brothers?" And pointing to his disciples, he said, "Here are my mother and my brothers! For whoever does the will of my Father in heaven is my brother and sister and mother."[33]

Through the eyes of faith we see everyone as our brother or sister in Christ. We have no relationships that are not family relationships; no interactions with others that are not family encounters. Not to acknowledge this in some way in our dealing with others is implicitly to deny what our faith tells us we are.

We may not be able to express this relationship in explicit terms, not knowing what others think or feel about it; but, we can always express it in some way, some appropriate way, that is dictated by what we believe:

• "Thanks for being so nice to me." • "Thanks for the smile." • "Be careful when you drive home; it's raining out there." • To a waitress: "You spend your whole day making people happy, don't you?" • To the security guard at the airport: "Thanks for keeping us safe." • To the janitor mopping the floor: "Thanks for keeping this place so clean; you do a great job. We appreciate it."

We can always show love in some form or another—as respect, as appreciation, as gratitude, as ordinary human concern. Not to show our faith, our hope, our love is implicitly to deny the life of grace that is within us and within others. That is to "hide our light under a bushel basket."[34]

> "Everyone therefore who acknowledges me before others, I also will acknowledge before my Father in heaven; but whoever denies me before others, I also will deny before my Father in heaven."[35]

If all of us who call God "Father" minister in this simple way to every person we meet, we will fill the world with love.

---

[33]*Matthew* 12:46-49.
[34]*Matthew* 5:14-16.
[35]*Matthew* 10:32-33.

And we will experience the fulfillment of Christ's promise, made to us at Baptism:

"I am the vine, you are the branches.
Those who abide in me and I in them bear much fruit."

Key Points:

- God has promised us, as he promised his chosen ones repeatedly in Scripture, a posterity. He has promised us that our ministry as priests will be life-giving. It will bear the lasting fruit of eternal life for others.

- There is only one Priest: Jesus Christ. But all who are "in Christ" by Baptism are "priests in the Priest."

- Baptism includes the promise of a union with Jesus like that of the branches with the vine, and of the fruitfulness in ministry that flows from that union.

- Ministry depends on "abiding" in Jesus, in living union with him, as the branch is united to the vine.

- Ministry is an experience of the person of Jesus within us, communicating his divine life through us to the persons to whom we minister.

- The key to ministry is surrender. We surrender by letting Christ express himself in and through our human words and actions.

- The essence of ministry is expression: giving physical expression to the invisible mystery of God's divine life within us.

- Graced self-expression is an act of "dying" to self. It is self-gift, vulnerability. Giving our "flesh for the life of the world," by surrendering our bodies to be the medium of Christ's self-expression.

- What transforms service to others into ministry is love—and specifically love expressed in our bodies as an expression of the divine love of Jesus Christ actively loving within us.

- When we are committed to doing this, every Mass becomes the most passionate expression of our lives. When the body and blood of Christ are lifted up, we say with him—to everyone in the world— "This is my body, offered for you."

QUESTIONS FOR REFLECTION AND DISCUSSION:

- Now that you have read this book, what does it mean to you that you became a priest through Baptism? How will this affect your behavior?

- How have you experienced "abiding" in Christ?

- Have you experienced surrendering to Christ by letting him express his truth, his love, through your actions?

- Do you find it hard to express your faith to others? To let God express his love to them through you? What makes this so difficult?

- How do we define "spousal love"? How is the mystery of spousal love for Christ included in Baptism?

- To what does the relationship of spousal love with Christ commit you?

- What does it promise?

- What is the goal of union with Christ and of the "spiritual marriage"?

A SUGGESTED KEY DECISION:

Concentrate on being loving to every person you encounter. Interact consciously with each one as a person and a brother or sister in Christ.

The Fifth Promise of Baptism
Victory

"Take courage; I have conquered the world!"
"As Christ was anointed . . . King,
so may you live always as a member of his body."[1]

In this chapter we ask: Are you aware that you are a king or steward of the kingship of Christ?

What does that mean? What mystery is enfolded in it? What promise does it hold out to you? To what does it commit you?

To answer those questions, we need to look into the mystery of the "Kingdom of God." Should we expect it here or hereafter? Is it something we ourselves are bringing about, or can we just wait for it to happen? What role does this play in the "new evangelization"?

All of this revolves around our baptismal commitment to stewardship. Rightly understood, stewardship may be our most total response to God.

> Strive first for the kingdom of God and his righteousness, and all these things will be given to you as well.

> The kingdom of heaven is like treasure hidden in a field, which someone found and hid; then in his joy he goes and sells all that he has and buys that field.[2]

It strikes me as strange that when my generation was growing up we heard little or nothing about the fundamental theme that characterized the preaching of Jesus: the Kingdom of God.

> Jesus came to Galilee, proclaiming the good news of God, and saying, "The time is fulfilled, and the Kingdom of God has come near; repent, and believe in the good news."[3]

We heard a lot about repenting, but to "repent" only meant to turn away from obvious sins, and it was in order to "get to heaven," not because the "Kingdom of God" had come near.

---

[1]*John* 16:33; *Rite of Baptism for Children*, no. 98.
[2]See *Matthew* 6:33; 13:44.
[3]*Mark* 1:14-15. See also *Matthew* 4:23; 9:35; *Luke* 8:1; *Acts* 8:12; 20:25; 28:31.

We were never told that we had been launched by Baptism into the work of bringing about a whole new way of thinking on earth, a whole new set of priorities and values, a whole new standard of behavior that would change everything people did—at home and in school, in church, business, social life, and family.

It was not impressed upon us that we were called to revolutionize our culture and the culture of every society on earth.

And there was no great emphasis or focus put on the promise that this would be accomplished; that the Kingdom would come. This didn't fire up our motivation on a day-to-day basis.

There also wasn't much emphasis on the "Good News." It was implicit, of course, in everything we learned from the Church, but we weren't really excited about how good our religion was. And we didn't experience it as news. Especially as the news that the "Kingdom of God" was about to come into being.

This is why the last four popes have been calling for a "new evangelization."

"Proclaiming the Good News of the Kingdom"

The ministry of Jesus is summarized twice by Matthew in identical words:

> Jesus went throughout Galilee, teaching in their synagogues and proclaiming the good news of the kingdom and curing every disease and every sickness among the people.[4]

Whatever people understood or Jesus actually meant by the "Kingdom of God," there is no doubt that it was the headline event of the Good News when he preached it. Jesus said repeatedly that this is what he came to preach: "I must proclaim the good news of the Kingdom of God to the other cities also; for I was sent for this purpose."[5]

The Kingdom was the subject of the private instruction he gave to his disciples: "To you it has been given to know the secrets of the Kingdom of heaven, but to them it has not been given." And this continued, even after his resurrection:

---

[4]*Matthew* 4:23, repeated word-for-word in 9:35.
[5]*Luke* 4:43. See also *Luke* 8:1; 9:11; 16:16; *Matthew* 4:17; 4:23; and 9:35.

After his suffering he presented himself alive to them by many convincing proofs, appearing to them during forty days and speaking about the Kingdom of God.[6]

The Kingdom is what he taught us to pray for: "When you pray, say: 'Father, hallowed be your name. Your Kingdom come. . . .'"[7]

The Kingdom was what he specifically promised to his disciples: "Do not be afraid, little flock, for it is your Father's good pleasure to give you the Kingdom. . . . and I confer on you, just as my Father has conferred on me, a kingdom, so that you may eat and drink at my table in my Kingdom."[8]

The warnings he gave were against attitudes and behavior that would keep people from entering into the Kingdom: "Not everyone who says to me, 'Lord, Lord,' will enter the Kingdom of heaven, but only the one who does the will of my Father in heaven . . . Truly I tell you, unless you change and become like children, you will never enter the Kingdom of heaven. . . . It will be hard for a rich person to enter the Kingdom of heaven."[9]

The Kingdom was the reward he promised to those who accepted his message: "The righteous will shine like the sun in the Kingdom of their Father. Let anyone with ears listen! . . . The Kingdom of heaven is like treasure hidden in a field, which someone found and hid; then in his joy he goes and sells all that he has and buys that field. . . . Then the king will say to those at his right hand, 'Come, you that are blessed by my Father, inherit the Kingdom prepared for you from the foundation of the world'. . . ."[10]

All of us who were anointed at Baptism to share in the mission of Jesus as Priest, Prophet, and King were promised a place in his Kingdom and given a share in his kingship.

Peter said, "Look, we have left our homes and followed you."

Jesus said to them, "Truly I tell you, there is no one who has left house or wife or brothers or parents or children, for the sake of the Kingdom of God, who will not get back very much more in this age and, in the age to come, eternal life."[11]

Paul wrote to Timothy: "If we endure, we will also reign with him."[12]

---

[6]*Matthew* 13:11; *Acts* 1:3.
[7]*Luke* 11:12.
[8]*Luke* 12:32; 22:29-30; 24:26.
[9]*Matthew* 7:21; 18:3; 19:14, 23-24. See also *Matthew* 21:28-43; 23:13.
[10]*Matthew* 13:43-44; 25:34.
[11]*Luke* 18:28-30.
[12]*2 Timothy* 2:12.

And the Book of Revelation: "You have made them to be a kingdom and priests serving our God, and they will reign on earth."[13]

Do we really believe that as stewards of the kingship of Christ we will "reign on earth"? Did Jesus promise this? Does it motivate anything we do?

HERE OR HEREAFTER?

Our temptation is to interpret this promise—and everything dealing with the "Kingdom"—as if it referred only to heaven or, at most, to the day when there will be "a new heaven and a new earth," after Jesus returns in glory at the end of the world.[14]

Mahalia Jackson once said, "Some people are so heavenly-minded they are no earthly good." In the same way, the "Kingdom of heaven" or "Kingdom of God" has become for us such an other-worldly concept that it hardly enters into our calculations about life on this planet. We work to "get to heaven," but not to establish the "Kingdom of heaven" on earth. We can be so "other-worldly" in our religion that we don't focus very seriously on what we should be accomplishing during the time of our "stewardship" in this world.

That is why our baptismal consecration to share in the anointing of Jesus as King may mean little to us. For the most part we just never think of ourselves as "stewards of his kingship." We are not excited by the announcement that "the Kingdom of God is at hand," because it doesn't seem to promise anything that touches our lives here and now. It doesn't motivate us to do much about the conditions of life in our society. The goal we focus on—"getting to heaven"—is not synonymous with realizing the Kingdom of God on this earth. So the proclamation that the "Kingdom of heaven is at hand" is not motivating news to us today.

So have we really heard the "good news"? Have we been authentically "evangelized"?

The proclamation of the Good News is that Jesus came to establish the Kingdom—here as well as hereafter. And at Baptism we were consecrated to work for it.

Furthermore, Christ promises us victory.

---

[13]*Revelation* 5:10.
[14]*Revelation* 21:1.

JESUS CAME AS KING

We think of Jesus as "Savior," "Teacher," and "Lord," but very seldom as "King."

In Jesus' own time, however, the role people gave to the "Messiah" was the role of king; specifically, "the king who would . . . bring Israel to its destiny. . . . The title Messiah-Christ meant kingship before it meant anything else; and everything suggests that to most Jews it meant nothing else." Why is it that in our time we seldom think or speak of Jesus as "King," and speak even less frequently about his "Kingdom"?[15]

One of the first things said of Jesus was that he was coming as King. This was the declaration the angel made to Mary before his birth:

> You will conceive in your womb and bear a son, and you will name him Jesus. He will be great, and will be called the Son of the Most High, and the Lord God will give to him the throne of his ancestor David. He will reign over the house of Jacob forever, and of his Kingdom there will be no end.

This was the title under which he was first introduced to the Gentiles:

> In the time of King Herod, after Jesus was born in Bethlehem of Judea, wise men from the East came to Jerusalem, asking, "Where is the child who has been born king of the Jews? For we observed his star at its rising, and have come to pay him homage."[16]

This was the title under which his future apostle Nathanael recognized him: "Rabbi, you are the Son of God! You are the King of Israel!" Jesus never repudiated the title, although he unequivocally refused to be the kind of king people wanted him to be: "When Jesus realized that they were about to come and take him by force to make him king, he withdrew again to the mountain by himself."[17]

This was the significance of his triumphal entry into Jerusalem. He entered as king, although it was to die as a criminal and "so enter into his glory."

The next day the great crowd that had come to the festival heard that Jesus was coming to Jerusalem. So they took branches of palm

---

[15]John McKenzie, *The Power and the Wisdom*, Bruce, 1965, pp. 73, 76.
[16]*Luke* 1:33; *Matthew* 2:1-2.
[17]*John* 1:49; 6:15.

trees and went out to meet him, shouting, "Hosanna! Blessed is the one who comes in the name of the Lord—the King of Israel!" Jesus found a young donkey and sat on it; as it is written: "Do not be afraid, daughter of Zion. Look, your king is coming, sitting on a donkey's colt!"

> Some of the Pharisees in the crowd said to him, "Teacher, order your disciples to stop." He answered, "I tell you, if these were silent, the stones would shout out."

> His disciples did not understand these things at first; but when Jesus was glorified, then they remembered that these things had been written of him and had been done to him.[18]

When he was delivered up to Pilate, "king" was the title he claimed—although not in the sense Pilate thought it had—and "king" was the title Pilate insisted on giving him:

> Pilate asked him, "So you are a king?" Jesus answered, "You say that I am a king. For this I was born, and for this I came into the world, to testify to the truth. Everyone who belongs to the truth listens to my voice."

> Pilate also had an inscription written and put on the cross. It read, "Jesus of Nazareth, the King of the Jews." Then the chief priests of the Jews said to Pilate, "Do not write, 'The King of the Jews,' but, 'This man said, I am King of the Jews.'"

> Pilate answered, "What I have written I have written."[19]

This is the title we share from our baptismal anointing as "prophets, priests, and kings." So we need to look at what the "kingship" of Jesus should mean to us today, and how we need to be involved in it.

WE ARE "KINGS IN THE KING"—STEWARDS OF HIS KINGSHIP

The Church insists today that a "constitutive element" of the process of evangelization—or "proclaiming the good news of the Kingdom"[20]—is to work for peace and justice in the world. This is an explicit fulfillment of our baptismal consecration as "kings." As the stewards of Christ's kingship on earth we commit ourselves to take responsibility for bringing every area and activity of human life on earth under the life-giving reign of Christ. We dedicate ourselves to transforming the social structures of this world.[21]

---

[18]*John* 12:13-16; *Luke* 19:39-40.
[19]*John* 18:37; 19:19-22.
[20]For this description of evangelization, see *Matthew* 4:23; 9:35; *Luke* 8:1; *Acts* 8:12.
[21]See Pope Paul VI, *On Evangelization in the Modern World*.

This is the emphatic teaching of the popes who have called for a "new evangelization"—both of the Church and by the Church—to respond to the reality of our times. Over the following pages you will see quoted material interspersed within the text. You may wish to refer to the footnotes for these sources. These many references are offered to you in order to show the major emphasis the Church continues to give to this theme of establishing Christ's Kingdom.[22]

PAPAL DOCTRINE

Jesus "first of all proclaims a kingdom, the Kingdom of God." This is "so important that, by comparison, everything else becomes 'the rest,' which is given in addition.[23] Only the Kingdom is absolute and it makes everything else relative."

The proclamation of the Kingdom is, for Christ's followers, a call to action. We are dedicated by Baptism to the cause of the Kingdom. There is no time for looking back, even less for "settling into laziness." There is work to be done. We must reject the temptation to reduce Christianity to a "privatized and individualistic spirituality." It is in contradiction to our Baptism to "remain indifferent" to the problems of our times or to be "disinterested in the welfare of our fellow human beings."[24]

Christians know, it is true, that "here we have no lasting city, but we are looking for the city that is to come." Our "citizenship is in heaven, and it is from there that we are expecting a Savior," waiting in "joyful hope for the coming of our Savior, Jesus Christ."[25]

---

[22]What follows is taken from Paul VI's Apostolic Exhortation *On Evangelization in the Modern World*, promulgated on December 8, 1975, and John Paul II's Apostolic Letter *At the Beginning of the New Millennium*, issued for the close of the Jubilee Year 2000. Most of what is given here is directly quoted from these documents, but instead of cluttering the text with an overwhelming number of quotation marks and references, I refer the reader to *Evangelii Nuntiandi*, numbers 8, 15, 20, 23; and to Novo Millennio Ineunte, numbers 5, 15, 46-51. These documents also refer repeatedly to the Second Vatican Council's documents, *Dogmatic Constitution on the Church* (Lumen Gentium), *Pastoral Constitution on the Church in the Modern World* (Gaudium et Spes), and *Decree on the Apostolate of the Laity* (Apostolicam Actuositatem). See also the Council's *Declaration on Religious Liberty* (Dignitatis Humanae), and *Decree on the Church's Missionary Activity* (Ad Gentes).
[23]*Matthew* 6:33.
[24]*Pastoral Constitution on the Church in the Modern World*, (Gaudium et Spes), no. 34.
[25]*Philippians* 3:20; *Hebrews* 13:14; and see the *Rite of Communion at Mass*.

However, this "eschatological tension" that keeps us living with one foot in this world and one foot in the next, in no way implies that we withdraw from "building history." On the contrary, "Christianity is a religion rooted in history!" It was "in the soil of history" that God made a covenant with Israel and prepared humanity for the birth of his Son "in the fullness of time."[26] Christ is the "foundation and center of history . . . its meaning and ultimate goal." His incarnation is the "pulsating heart of time, the mysterious hour in which the Kingdom of God came to us, indeed took root in our history, as the seed destined to become a great tree."[27]

The Kingdom, then, is not just something we will enjoy after death; it is something to be realized in history, in our world, in our time. The Kingdom, in fact, is "the meaning of history and the light of life's journey." Christians find—and make—their way in this world in the light of the Kingdom they are working to establish.

THE TRANSFORMATION OF CULTURES

When we say "Kingdom," we are talking about a transformation of society itself. "What matters is to evangelize human culture and cultures, not in a purely decorative way, as it were, by applying a thin veneer, but in a vital way, in depth and right to their very roots."[28]

A culture is made up of a whole complex of attitudes, values, priorities, ways of thinking and behaving that have come to be accepted as normal in a particular society. A culture is something people "fit into," something they conform to more than they realize, even when, in one area or another, they see themselves as "non-conformist." We cannot escape the influence of culture. "Culture" is everything we have learned from others in our society, good and bad—from our family, school, church, social circle, professional milieu, and political climate. From parents, siblings, preachers, teachers, friends, and associates. Culture seeps into and gives its taste to everything we are and experience, like rum in a rum cake. We have no idea how we would experience ourselves or any aspect of our lives without the influence of cultural conditioning. We can't even imagine how we would experience the most basic ingredients of our consciousness if

---

[26]*Galatians* 4:4.
[27]See *Mark* 1:15; 4:30-32.
[28]*The Church in the Modern World* (Gaudium et Spes), no. 53.

we were in some "pure state," unformed and unaffected by culture. Our sense of security and success, competitiveness, defensive instincts, sexuality, relationship with others—all of these have been both formed and deformed by the influence of the culture we grew up in and absorbed. That influence is immeasurable and, in great part, undetectable. For the most part, we just don't know why we feel, think, and act as we spontaneously do.

Establishing the Kingdom is a matter of bringing people to greater personal freedom by making them aware of their unexamined cultural attitudes and values, challenging them, offering alternatives for them to accept in conscious, deliberate choice.

The proclamation of the Kingdom "only reaches full development when it is listened to, accepted and assimilated" in personal choice. The Kingdom is only authentic when it arouses a genuine, personal adherence "to a program of life, a life henceforth transformed—in a word, adherence to the 'new world,' to the new state of things, to the new manner of being, of living, of living in community, which the Gospel sets in motion."

RESPECT FOR WHAT IS NATURAL

The Kingdom brings everything to the level of the divine without destroying or distorting any natural human values. This is "not a case of imposing on non-believers a vision based on faith, but of interpreting and defending the values rooted in the very nature of the human person." The work of the Kingdom does no disservice to natural institutions, but is rather a "service to culture, politics, the economy and the family." This is because in God's Kingdom (which is the Kingdom of the Creator as well as of the Redeemer), "the fundamental principles upon which depend the destiny of human beings and the future of civilization will be everywhere respected."

CHRISTIAN SOCIAL ACTION

Establishing the Kingdom of God is different from helping the poor. The Church cannot be authentically herself without service to the poor, of course, and to the rich as well, because the love Jesus preached "of its nature opens out into a service that is universal; it inspires in us a commitment to practical and concrete love for every human being. . . . No one can be excluded from our love, since through his Incarnation the Son of God has united himself in some fashion with every person." But for Christians there is "a special presence of Christ in the poor," which requires the Church to make a "preferential option" for them.[29]

But helping the poor is not enough. To establish the Kingdom of God we have to address the causes of poverty and of all the elements in society that inflict distress and diminishment on human beings. This directs our attention to the Church's well-known and undeniable "contribution to the social question, which has now assumed a global dimension."[30]

Among the "many needs which demand a compassionate response from Christians," the papal documents alert us to "the contradictions of an economic, cultural, and technological progress which offers immense possibilities to a fortunate few, while leaving millions of others. . . . in living conditions far below the minimum demanded by human dignity."

How can it be, the popes ask, that even today there are still people dying of hunger? Condemned to illiteracy? Lacking the most basic medical care? Without a roof over their heads?

The modern Church is painfully aware of a "scenario of poverty" that is extending beyond traditional forms to confront us with "newer patterns" in which even financially affluent sectors and groups are "threatened by despair at the lack of meaning in their lives, by drug addiction, by fear of abandonment in old age or sickness, by marginalization or social discrimination."

We "cannot remain indifferent":

- to the "ecological crisis which is making vast areas of our planet uninhabitable and hostile to humanity";
- to the "problems of peace, threatened by the specter of catastrophic wars";
- to resurgent "contempt for the fundamental human rights of so many people, especially children."

---

[29] *The Church in the Modern World* (Gaudium et Spes).
[30] *ibid.*

All of these are the challenge of establishing the Kingdom of God on our earth, in our time, by our efforts aided by the empowering grace of the light and love of God. Today the "tradition of charity" calls for greater resourcefulness. Now is the time for a "new creativity" in love.

This is a call to action. The Christian message risks being distorted and "submerged in the ocean of words which daily engulfs us in today's society of mass communications." But the proclamation of the Gospel, which is certainly a "charity of words," demands for its effectiveness the "charity of works." More than ever before, to stand in prophetic witness before the world, the Church must measure up to Christ's own criterion: "You will know them by their fruits"; that is, by their deeds.[31]

Action to bring about justice and peace on earth is what the popes are calling "the greatest and most effective presentation of the good news of the Kingdom."

"Take Courage; I Have Conquered the World!"

In seeking to establish the "Kingdom of God" on earth, Christians are taking on the task of transforming all the cultures of the world:

- Making business and politics divine in purpose and policies while leaving their natures intact.
- Freeing family and social life to be experienced interaction with God in human intercourse—an experience of God incarnate, indwelling and expressing himself in ourselves and through others.
- Healing our society's unchallenged—even unrecognized—attitudes and behavior that have veered off toward destructiveness and distortion, mediocrity and meaninglessness.
- Establishing the "reign of God" in every area and activity of human life on earth.

An eternal and universal kingdom:

a kingdom of truth and life,
a kingdom of holiness and grace,
a kingdom of justice, love, and peace.[32]

---

[31]See *Matthew* 7:16.
[32]See the *Preface for the Mass of Christ the King.*

92

David taking on Goliath. Dreaming the impossible dream. This is the scope of the Kingdom:

> For the Church, evangelizing means bringing the Good News into all the strata of humanity, and through its influence transforming humanity from within and making it new: "Now I am making the whole of creation new."

> Though independent of cultures the Gospel and evangelization are . . . capable of permeating all [cultures] without becoming subject to any one of them. They have to be regenerated by an encounter with the Gospel.

What this means in practice is "affecting and as it were upsetting, through the power of the Gospel, the human race's criteria of judgment, determining values, points of interest, lines of thought, sources of inspiration, and models of life, which are in contrast with the Word of God and the plan of salvation."

This puts special focus on the "lay apostolate."

The proclamation of the Good News through this "new creativity in love"—a culture-challenging love carried out in action—is in a very special way "the specific vocation of the laity," who are explicitly called and consecrated by Baptism to "seek the Kingdom of God by engaging in temporal affairs and by ordering them according to the plan of God."[33]

A daunting task. But its accomplishment is a promise of our Baptism. We were consecrated "kings in the King" who arrived proclaiming, "The Kingdom of God is at hand." To empower us, Jesus said, "Take courage; I have conquered the world!"[34]

We need courage to dedicate ourselves to the transformation of the world. And given the apparent hopelessness of the task, we need divine courage.

And we need to dedicate ourselves without reserve. Totally.

This calls for the total gift of ourselves to God and to the world. Another word for this is total "abandonment." This is both the foundation and the goal of our baptismal consecration as kings or stewards of the kingship of Christ. It is, in a very particular way, the laity's path to perfection.

---

[33]See the Second Vatican Council, "*Dogmatic Constitution on the Church*" (Lumen Gentium), no. 31.
[34]*John* 16:33.

Stewardship, Leadership, and Abandonment

A "steward" is one who manages the property of another. The steward's principal concern is to be "faithful." This fidelity consists in two things: renunciation of all private self-interest, and responsibility (exercising leadership) in promoting the interests of the owner in every decision about the use and disposition of the owner's goods.

To be a steward of Christ's kingship is to exercise responsible leadership in managing everything that comes from Christ, belongs to Christ, or was created for Christ, in such a way that it contributes to the establishment of the Kingdom of God on earth.

This includes everything.

Everything comes from Christ as source. At the beginning of time, "all things in heaven and on earth were created . . . through him and for him."[35]

Everything belongs to Christ as King. Jesus said before he died: "All things have been handed over to me by my Father."[36]

The true "mystery of God's will," that he "set forth in Christ, as a plan for the fullness of time," is to "bring all things in the heavens and on earth into one under Christ's headship."[37]

In Christ, at the end of time, all things in heaven and on earth will be "united," "gathered up," "summed up," "recapitulated," "brought together under a single head." This is Paul's vision of the radiant glory, shrouded in mystery, of the "end time."

The goal of all creation is Jesus Christ himself, the "perfect man," the body of Christ, head and members, all of humanity brought to the fullness of perfection.

> The gifts he gave were . . . for building up the body of Christ, until we all become one in faith and in the knowledge of God's Son, and form that perfect man who is Christ come to full stature.[38]

---

[35]*Colossians* 1:16.
[36]*Matthew* 11:27.
[37]*Ephesians* 1:10.
[38]*Ephesians* 4:11-13.

To be a "faithful steward," then, is to give, to surrender, to abandon all that one has and is to Christ and then to manage in his name and for his Kingdom everything over which we have any control on this earth.

Stewardship is total giving, and total giving is stewardship. By Baptism we "died" to this world in order to live only as the risen body of Christ on earth. We gave up, in the most radical way, everything we have in this world: all our possessions, all societal claims from human relationships, life itself. Then God placed them all in our hands again, not to own, but to manage for him. By Baptism we became "stewards" of all that is under our control. Our preoccupation is to use and manage our time, energies, talents, relationships, and any possessions that are legally ours, in the way that is most according to God's will, the way that will contribute most to the establishment of his Kingdom on earth. Literally, we own nothing. We simply manage what is God's.[39]

This is the foundational reality of our baptismal consecration as kings or stewards of the kingship of Christ (and of all our baptismal commitments). By this consecration we are committed to work for the establishment of God's reign on earth, but the foundation of that commitment is the total abandonment of all that we have and are to God. To be a steward is to have nothing of one's own, but to manage everything for God. To accept this is to enter into a state of total abandonment to God.

To arrive at this is the fifth promise and purpose of our Baptism.

FROM SURRENDER TO ABANDONMENT

If we don't take the comparison too literally, we can compare the surrender we make in our ministry as priests with the abandonment that characterizes our stewardship as kings. We may use for a guide a comparison St. Teresa of Avila makes between the spiritual "betrothal" and the "spiritual marriage" in her *Interior Castle*.

Teresa writes that the difference between the spiritual betrothal and the spiritual marriage is that, in the betrothal, union is not constant.

---

[39]This is explicit in the Gospel. Jesus says that all who want to follow him must "die" to: •possessions: *Matthew* 19:21-24; *Luke* 14:33; even to such basics as the need for shelter: *Matthew* 8:19-20; •relationships: *Luke* 12:53; 14:26; 18:28-30; *Matthew* 8:21-22; *Mark* 8:38; 10:29-30; •marriage: *Luke* 20:34-35; •life itself: *Matthew* 16:24-25; 18:7-9; *John* 12:25.

It comes and goes. And we can say there is a parallel to this in the difference between surrendering ourselves to let Jesus within us give himself to others through us in ministry—which still takes place in individual actions—and abandoning ourselves totally to God and to the Church in stewardship. In ministry, we give ourselves to God and to others in distinct actions. In total abandonment, we simply give over all that we have and are, whole and entire, to be used for God's service.

> The spiritual betrothal is different [from spiritual marriage], for the two [parties] often separate. . . . Let us say that the union is like the joining of two wax candles to such an extent that the flame coming from them is but one, or that the wick, the flame, and the wax are all one. But afterwards one candle can be easily separated from the other and there are two candles. . . .
>
> In the spiritual marriage the union is like what we have when rain falls from the sky into a river or fount; all is water, for the rain that fell from heaven cannot be divided or separated from the water of the river.[40]

Or like the water mingled with the wine at Mass.

We surrender in many different acts. But when we abandon ourselves as stewards to the work of the Kingdom, there is nothing left to surrender. All is given. Once and for all.

This is expressed in the prayer through which St. Ignatius brings our response to God to its climax in the last meditation of his *Spiritual Exercises*:

> *Take, Lord, and receive all my liberty,*
> *my memory, my understanding, and my entire will—*
> *all that I have and possess.*
> *You have given all to me. To you, Lord, I return it.*
> *All is yours. Dispose of it wholly according to your will.*
> *Give me your love and your grace.*
> *That is enough for me.*[41]

This is the "prayer of stewardship." To say this prayer from the heart is to arrive—on a personal, individual level, at least—at the victory promised in Baptism. It is to enter into the Kingdom by abandoning ourselves totally to the work of establishing the Kingdom for others.

---

[40]*Interior Castle*, "Seventh Dwelling Place," ch. 2, no. 4.
[41]*The Spiritual Exercises*, no. 234. Translation by Fr. George Ganss, S.J., Loyola University Press, 1992.

A Simple Suggestion: One Change at a Time

A simple way to live out our consecration as stewards of the kingship of Christ—simple, but not simplistic—is just to keep trying to change things you see around you that need changing. Little things, big things, whatever is at hand. From picking up a piece of paper on the floor to starting a new political party.

A key word here is "trying."

To be a faithful steward we do not have to succeed in what we do. We just have to be faithful in trying.

We can try by ourselves, as individuals. We can try to enlist the support of others. We can try to convince authorities that they should adopt a certain policy for the whole community—or even declare a change of course. We can try to persuade other individuals to do something in a different way. We may not have the authority or the power to bring these changes about. We just have the responsibility to try.

We can always change the way we ourselves do things. Change begins at home.

Responsibility begins with noticing. And noticing is a matter of mindset. We notice things we are concerned about, things we think are "our business." If we think something is "not our business," we tend to "keep our nose out of it." We don't pay attention to it.

As stewards of the kingship of Christ, we see everything in this world as "our business." We have accepted responsibility for trying to establish the reign of God over every area and activity of human life on earth. We are alert to anything and everything that needs changing. Everything destructive. Everything distorted. Everything that could be better. Everything that could enhance human life on the planet.

We don't invade others' privacy. But we are alert to the effect individual actions have on the community as a whole. Or on the human race. There is profound, mystical truth in the meditation of John Donne:

> No man is an island entire of itself; every man is a piece of the continent, a part of the main. If a clod be washed away by the sea, Europe is the less, as well as if a promontory were, as well as if a manor of thy friend's or of thine own were. Any man's death diminishes me, because I am involved in mankind, and therefore never send to know for whom the bell tolls; it tolls for thee.[42]

---

[42]Meditations, XVII, from John Donne, *Devotions Upon Emergent Occasions*, 1624.

This is a charter for stewardship. It is a foundational concept for Christian leadership.

The mystery is the Kingdom of God. The promise is victory. To help bring it about is a "constitutive element" of our way of life.

> Then I heard every creature in heaven and on earth and under the earth and in the sea, and all that is in them, singing, "To the one seated on the throne and to the Lamb be blessing and honor and glory and might forever and ever!"[43]

KEY POINTS:

- The "headline event" Jesus preached was that the "Kingdom of God" is at hand. This was the "Good News."

- Our temptation is to interpret this promise as if it referred only to heaven or to the end of the world, when Jesus returns in glory.

- Our baptismal consecration to share in the anointing of Jesus as King means we are "stewards of his kingship."

- As the stewards of Christ's kingship on earth, we commit ourselves to take responsibility for bringing every area and activity of human life on earth under the life-giving reign of Christ. We dedicate ourselves to transforming the cultures and social structures of this world.

- This is the emphatic teaching of the popes who have called for a "new evangelization"—both of the Church and by the Church—to respond to the reality of our times.

- Action to bring about justice and peace on earth is what the popes are calling "the greatest and most effective presentation of the good news of the Kingdom."

- This is in a very special way "the specific vocation of the laity," who are called and consecrated by Baptism to "seek the Kingdom of God by engaging in temporal affairs and by ordering them according to the plan of God."

- We need courage to dedicate ourselves to the transformation of the world. And given the apparent hopelessness of the task, we need divine courage. This is the divine gift of hope.

---

[43]*Revelation* 5:13.

- The work of the Kingdom calls for the total gift of ourselves to God and to the world. Another word for this is total "abandonment." This is both the foundation and the goal of our baptismal consecration as kings or stewards of the kingship of Christ.

- A "steward" is one who manages the property of another. The steward's principal concern is to be "faithful." This fidelity consists in two things: renunciation of all private self-interest, and responsibility (exercising leadership) in promoting the interests of the owner in every decision about the use and disposition of the owner's goods.

- Stewardship is total giving, and total giving is stewardship. By Baptism we "died" to this world in order to live only as the risen body of Christ on earth. We gave up in the most radical way everything we have in this world: all our possessions, all societal claims from human relationships, life itself. Then God placed them all in our hands again, not to own, but to manage for him.

- To be a "faithful steward" is to give, to surrender, to abandon to Christ all that one has and is and then to manage in his name and for his Kingdom everything over which we have any control on this earth.

- To be a steward of Christ's kingship is to exercise responsible leadership in such a way that everything contributes to the establishment of the Kingdom of God on earth.

Questions For Reflection and Discussion:

- What does it mean to you now to work to establish the "Kingdom of God" on earth?

- Do you see changes that need to be made in your own family life? (Don't mention them if they are private). Social life? Business or professional life?

- What motivates you to work for change on earth?

- What gives you hope when the "Kingdom" seems to be a losing proposition?

A Suggested Key Decision:

Begin by just "noticing" what could be improved in your own environment: at home, at work, in your neighborhood, or city.

Try each day to change one thing, no matter how small.

Father David Knight has spent 50 years of priesthood ministering as a pastor, high school teacher, professor of theology, missioner, and retreat director. He lives in Memphis, TN, and runs His Way Center for Spiritual Growth. Father Knight teaches in the Christian Brothers University Graduate Program in Catholic Studies and the Diocese of Memphis Institute for Liturgy and Spirituality. He is retired as pastor of Sacred Heart Catholic Church.